A Practical Guide to Autism

Support for Parents and Carers

Dr Andy Evans

Pavilion
PUBLISHING

A Practical Handbook to Autism:
A Support Guide for Parents and Carers

© Pavilion Publishing & Media

The author has asserted his rights in accordance with the Copyright, Designs and Patents Act (1988) to be identified as the author of this work.

Published by:
Pavilion Publishing and Media Ltd
Blue Sky Offices, 25 Cecil Pashley Way, Shoreham by Sea,
West Sussex, BN43 5FF

Tel: +44 (0)1273 434943
Email: info@pavpub.com
Web: www.pavpub.com

Published 2024

All rights reserved. No part of this publication may be reproduced, stored in a retrieval system, or transmitted in any form or by any means, electronic, mechanical, photocopying, recording or otherwise, without prior permission in writing of the publisher and the copyright owners.

A catalogue record for this book is available from the British Library.

ISBN: 978-1-803883-91-5

Pavilion Publishing and Media is a leading publisher of books, training materials and digital content in mental health, social care and allied fields. Pavilion and its imprints offer must-have knowledge and innovative learning solutions underpinned by sound research and professional values.

Author: Dr Andy Evans
Copyeditor: Mike Benge
Cover design: Emma Dawe and Phil Morash, Pavilion Publishing and Media Ltd
Page layout and typesetting: Phil Morash and Emma Dawe, Pavilion Publishing and Media Ltd
Printing: Independent Publishers Group (IPG)

To

Jacqueline, Elizabeth and Anthony

Contents

Acknowledgements 1

Preface 3

Introduction 5

Chapter 1: Parent or carer? 9
    Are you a carer? 9
    Mindset 12
        What if? 14
        Confrontation 15
        Crises or boulders 17
    Welfare 18
    Milestones 23
    My list of dos 24
    Who is the expert? 25
    Words of caution 26

Chapter 2: About autism 29
    What is autism? 30
        Types of autism 31
        Needs 32
        The professionals 32
        An autistic perspective 35
        What carers think 36
        Bundles 38
        Social rules 40
    Terminology explained 41
        The spectrum 41
        Abstract concepts 43
        Special interests 44
        Perception, literalism and logic 45

- Shutdown/meltdown 46
- Masking 48
- Stimming 50
- Burnout 51
- Executive functioning 52
- Neurodivergence and neurodiversity 55
- Hyperlexia 56
- Monotropism 56
- Apraxia 56
- Selective mutism 57
- Echolalia 59
- Alexithymia 60

Things to be aware of 61
- Eye contact 61
- Sensory overload 62
- Food and eating disorders 63
- Sleep 65
- Non-verbal autism 67
- Interoception 68
- Anger rumination 68
- Inappropriate behaviour 68
- Early death 69
- Change 72
- Refusal 78
- Pain 82
- Fixations 84
- Unintended consequences 84

Invisibility and disability 85
- Is autism a disability? 86
- Social interaction 88
- Loneliness 89
- Acceptance/Awareness days 90

Prevalence 91

Origins and myths 94
- A short history of autism 94
- Culture 95
- Genetics and heritability 98
- Myths 99

Chapter 3: Practical advice 101
Diagnosis 101
- When you first notice 102
- Telling your loved one 104
- The process 105
- The aftermath 107
- Private or NHS 107

Listening (and reading) 109
Education 111
- Selecting a school 111
- Accessing support 113
- Forms 117
- School environment and culture 118
- Examinations 124
- Post-school education 126

Healthcare 126
- Communication 127
- Gatekeepers 128
- Environment 130
- Prevention 131
- Mental health 131
- We know best 133

The law and knowing your rights 134
- Equality and discrimination 134
- Police 135
- Courts 137

Mental Health Act and suicide 138
Ageing 140
- My plan 141
- Write a will 141
- Paperwork 142
- Other things 144
- Final thoughts 144

Employment 145
- Recruitment agencies 146
- Interviews 146
- Types of working 148
- Unemployment 149

- Discrimination 150
- Reasonable adjustments 152
- Money.. 153
  - Social security... 154
  - Trusts 158
  - Power of Attorney 160
  - Discounts 162
  - Direct payments 163
  - Inheritance 164
  - Carer access 165
- Travel and holidays 165
- Local authorities 168
  - Statutory duties...170
  - Organisational structure...171
  - Contacting your LA 172
  - Accessing services 173
  - Carers assessment and reviews 173
  - Homelessness 174

Chapter 4: Building understanding 177
- Reading and listening... 178
  - Books and journals... 178
  - Social media and websites 179
  - Blogs and podcasts..181
- Words matter..181
  - Labels... 182
  - Insults 183
  - Person first 184
  - Unintended phrases.. 185
  - Managing anxiety 186
  - Aspergers.. 188
  - Functioning 188
  - Never-use terms and phrases 189
  - Kindness... 190
  - Puzzle piece...191
- Therapies 191
  - How to access therapy 192
  - Apps 194
  - CBT 194
  - ABA/PBS therapy 196

    Other therapy options 197
    Dialectical therapy 197
    Acceptance and commitment therapy 198
    Son-Rise therapy 198
    Horse-riding therapy 198
    Alternative medicine 198

Chapter 5: Building resilience **201**
   How 203
   Coping mechanisms 204
   Planning 205
   Feedback 207

Chapter 6: Lived experience **209**
   Luke 210
   Simon 212
   Keith Ridley 213
   Graham 214
   Leanne and Jordan 216
   Paul Ridley 218
   Andreas 219

Chapter 7: Conclusion **221**
   The takeaways 222
   That Mindset 222
   Final words 223

Glossary **225**
References **226**

Acknowledgements

My journey with autism, as an unpaid carer, has been made up of many conversations with professionals, other parents and carers, teachers and autistic people. Sometimes, these conversations were about my loved one, Joe, or about autism, or the cul-de-sacs we sometimes found ourselves in. Each conversation moved us forward.

Many of the quotes or paraphrased quotes included in this work have come from these conversations, whether face to face, from social media threads (mostly X – formerly Twitter – and WhatsApp) and emails. On many occasions, the conversations were fleeting, and sometimes I would make a mental or written note of what I learnt or what they said. Many times, I was looking for a solution or greater understanding and would often forget or fail to record their names, let alone seek their permission to reuse their words or ideas. Many times, I was desperate to find a virtual ladder to get out the hole we had found ourselves in.

I hope everyone will accept that my only intention is to help parents to understand their autistic loved ones better, to avoid the cul-de-sacs, and not to endure the endless battles with officialdom we have had to fight. Please accept my apologies if I have not acknowledged your individual and unique contribution. Please accept my deepest thanks. Where possible, I have asked permission to include the thoughts of others. Please understand many people have wished to remain anonymous or to be acknowledged under a pseudonym.

Some of the ideas and explanations in this guide have come from Beth Wilson, Gary Freeman, Paul Ridley, Marie Martin, Andrea Heywood, Jill

Acknowledgements

Jablonski, Deb Wood, the late Mr Pant, Anna Rebowska, 'The Tattered Fox', Susan Phelps, Claire, Kate Alton, JE, Marie Burgin, 'Supertes', Sarah Davey, Becky Stack, Angela Whitehead, 'Activist Lawyer', Catharine Fairbairn, 'BinkyBrewer' and my family. Some of the carers who have contributed are autistic or have ADHD.

I would like to thank the following autistic people for their contributions: 'Luke', 'Simon', Zak Martin, Keith Ridley, Mr Chamberlain, Jon Adams, 'Sarah', 'Abbey', 'Safari', 'FelineLover', 'The Tolerant Dinosaur', 'Autjoy', Vale Giovanardi, Helen B, Amanda, Rebecca, Caroline F, Kyle Morgan, William Rice, Sophie Porritt, Kev Brown, Jess Plant, Edward Philips, Alicia Painter, and my own tour guide of all things autistic.

I wish to acknowledge four remarkable professionals who have made my journey possible: Jenny Wilson, our first NHS clinical psychologist, who made a significant difference in the early days of this journey; Mrs Julie Cawthorpe, an SLT-based SENCO at St Pauls Senior School, a lady who listened and made the mountain come to us; the late Miss Janet Probert and Mrs Emma Chamberlain. All very extraordinary ladies who have made everything possible.

A huge shout is needed for Nanny P, my dad and brother, for always listening to me when my black dog bites.

Preface

My name is Andy. A long time ago, I discovered a totally different way of seeing and feeling, following the birth of my son, Joe. Joe is autistic. Joe has an almost photographic memory and a very perceptive way of being in the world.

As Joe grew, I found I needed more information to understand what clinicians and other professionals were saying. I needed the information to ensure I was doing the best for Joe. That need has grown into an interest or hobby about all things to do with autism, additional educational needs, and dyslexia. I run a few automated Twitter sites that share this accumulated 'knowledge' with the world.

Over the years, we have supported other families sharing a similar journey with autism. Autism may initially appear scary, especially when you don't know much about it. Most parents don't know where to turn and many feel overwhelmed. As I supported more people, I soon realised that most were suffering from too much or too little information. Sometimes, the more information they had the less they understood.

To simplify the support and help myself so I didn't end up repeating myself, I wrote a short guide briefly explaining autism, the SEN system, basic social security, and some of the jargon. That guide has grown into this book.

This book is aimed at people who have just been invited to share a journey with autism, whether parents, grandparents, siblings or newly diagnosed autistic people. Unlike many authors, I have no formal qualifications in autism or dyslexia but have over about 30 years of lived experience. I believe that lived experience imparts a 'hands-on' knowledge that some professionals lack. I feel I may have an insight that is probably helpful to other parents or carers and some recently diagnosed autistic people.

Introduction

Most people first encounter autism when a clinician, psychologist or teacher first mentions the 'A' word. Initially, you may feel overwhelmed, your mind may race, and your future may suddenly become very uncertain. Please understand that this is not uncommon. A formal diagnosis or a professional suggestion of autism doesn't change your child. Your child is the same and all that has changed is your perception of the future.

You will probably have read stories of other people's journeys on social media and in the press. You will have noticed most of the stories were always negative, with the worst possible tragic outcomes. Many will either be painful or full of despair. Think about these posts initially as you would people moaning about their recent holiday experiences on TripAdvisor: as you may have noticed, people only tend to post hotel reviews when something has gone 'wrong'.

This journey will reshape you, scare you and at times devour you, so focus on the horizon and take your time. There will be times when you will need to shout at the world. At times, autism may appear relentless, and seem to take no prisoners. Autism will appear to find your weaknesses and exploit them. Please understand, it is simply your brain trying to make sense of reality and adjust to that new way of seeing the world. A new way you will quickly grow to appreciate.

Raising an autistic child is no different to raising a non-autistic child; it is a lifelong endeavour. As you are probably aware, children don't come with manuals. All parenting journeys teach you new skills and you always learn to be adaptable. Believe what your instincts tell you. Above all, believe in you and your loved one. You will soon realise that you have got this.

When I began this journey, there was little awareness and very little acceptance of autism. Over the years, things have gradually improved because of people who have made this journey before you. There have been positive changes in legislation that give your loved one enhanced rights, and better access to services and support. Mandatory training of medics in autism and learning disabilities is in place, and soon may extend to include all teachers and teaching staff.

Many parents will receive little signposting or a discussion of the next steps following a diagnosis. Many are desperate for meaningful information, including where to start.

While Google is useful, it can also direct parents to resources that are out of date or which may be harmful if read without context. For example, searching for therapies usually brings up ABA/PBS, vaccine injury, miracle cures etc. Context is very important with autism.

This book aims to fill the information void with discussion and facts from carers and autistic people so you can make better choices and avoid the cul-de-sacs many of us initially go down. The aim is to inform without offering biased opinions.

Most carers I speak to are unaware of the depth and breadth of the community they have joined; most are initially unaware of the services they may need, their loved one's rights, and the financial and moral support they can access. A recurring refrain that comes up in my conversations is, 'No one told us'. The guide aims to address that directly.

This book provides an overview of autism, including descriptions of each trait from an autistic point of view, and a supporting description from a non-autistic perspective, comorbidities (other bundled conditions) and why these need to be remembered. It also explores the cultural and historical basis of autism, because this shapes society's attitude and the current thinking about autism.

The book has an overview of NHS services, Local Authority (LA) services, DWP benefits, and education. Each comes with a discussion of how to access the services in a timely manner. There is an overview of some therapies and a discussion of the downsides and upsides of some of them.

While most of this is loosely based on my own journey and therefore contains my own biases, assumptions, and intolerances, please understand, it is not about me. Other carers and autistic people have made valuable contributions and observations. Please also understand that the law, processes, social security, medical systems, and legislation described and discussed in this guide are applicable to the UK only (please note legislation and practice change). Please do not take discussions as advice. Always consult appropriate professionals. I hope this guide is helpful and provides some illumination for your journey ahead.

Chapter 1:
Parent or carer?

Think about the conversations you have with other people for a moment. In the UK, you might talk about the weather or your family, and in particular your children. Most people take pride in sharing stories of their children, especially ones that involve milestones, like the first time they called you 'dad', when they graduated etc. It is something that we instinctively share even with strangers. It's what parents do.

Becoming a parent changes your life, hopefully for the better. Many of the chores and routines in your life change when you become a parent. Your work and life balance become more important, and your socialising evolves. When you become a parent, you begin a journey of caring, filled with the joy of those milestones.

A journey shared with autism is no different: it is equally filled with joy, happiness and contentment, proud milestones to share. The only difference is that, on occasion, you may have to dig a little deeper.

Are you a carer?

Many people describe themselves by the dominant activities (or contexts) in their lives. Some will say, 'I am a policeman and a dad'. A few will simply say they are 'mum'. Most people have more than one 'hat', as I describe them.

Chapter 1: Parent or carer?

I have many hats, including 'engineer', 'dad', 'Viking' and 'carer'. My 'Viking' hat is worn when I deal with bureaucracy, but I will come to that later. My 'engineer' hat is the one I wear when working. My 'carer' hat is the one I wear all the time.

How do you know if you are a carer? For me, you become a carer the first moment you advocate for someone else. Whether it's talking to a teacher about your loved one's needs, accompanying your mum to the GP, or just reaching out to your council for home help. At that moment you become a carer.

Some people think being a carer is looking after an elderly relative and all that this entails. For example, it may be doing their weekly shopping, daily checking in by telephone, accompanying them to an occasional hospital appointment or running the hoover around their house. Some families may share these 'chores'. Some may have to dig deeper and become Power of Attorneys to safeguard their relative's finances as they decline and maintain their home and their quality of life. It is a role you generally have time to evolve into. In contrast, when you support an autistic loved one, you need to hit the ground running.

Many government and similar organisations define being 'a carer' in terms of contact hours, repetitive tasks etc. For example, the UK government provides some deferred and current financial support in the form of Carer's

Credit and Carer's Allowance if contact hours thresholds are met (35 hours). The NHS and many charities describe a carer as anyone who looks after someone, who cannot cope without their support, unpaid.

For me, the contact hours and 'cannot cope' definitions fail to adequately describe being a carer for invisible disabilities like autism. For example, an arthritic elderly relative has needs that can be more easily defined and quantified. Invisible disabilities are harder to quantify into contact time as you are always on standby. 'Coping' is a very divisive concept when invisible disabilities are involved.

Some carers become what I call 'sandwich' carers because they care for two or more people. This can be difficult if there is more than one location, and the carer has to share their time by need. Sandwich caring can include supporting someone by telephone. You'd be surprised what you can do with a telephone and the internet. Typically, a sandwich carer could be supporting an elderly parent and a child. Even if you have siblings, you may find yourself alone in this task with little support from them. It is worth bearing in mind they won't know you are struggling unless you tell them. Sadly, they may choose to leave you to deal with what can seem an impossible task. At times, you may feel guilty for prioritising the needs of those you support, but remember that your child should always be the priority.

For me, a carer is simply someone who prioritises their loved ones needs over their own. Some may say that sounds very much like a parent, but please pause for a moment and compare what you do with other parents you know. Do you notice any significant differences?

It is important that you remember that, as a carer, you have rights. (Carers UK, 2024, has a detailed list of these rights.) Some of these rights will be statutory and others may be contractual with your employer. Most of these rights exist to give you some flexibility and some protection from the discrimination you may face because you are a carer.

You have the right to ask for flexible working, but you are limited to one request a year. Your request can only be rejected for a sound business reason. Additionally, you have the right to reasonable time off in emergencies.

There will be times when you may struggle to juggle work, caring and having a life. The Carers' Leave Act (2024) give you access to five days of no-questions-asked unpaid leave from your work. While it is not perfect, this may help you deal with medical and DWP appointments and those 'best interests' meetings you must attend without worry.

When you begin this caring journey, you may only see a hard road ahead, but many parents and carers have lots of positives to report. Many describe the extraordinary bond and trust they have with their children and how proud they are of themselves.

As JE explains, being a carer gives her, 'Lots of time with the children, getting true affection (not faked to get something), learning about oneself and the children themselves'.

Marie Burgin similarly explains that, 'Due to very little outside support, official or otherwise, I am extremely proud of the bond I have with my children (both deaf, 'severe' autism & LD). I am also finally proud of myself (takes some admitting) for getting us through the sh*t show that is LA services.'

'Supertes' adds, 'Being able to "need" to know your children so well you learn foresight like no other – eventually the inner strength & stoicism becomes second nature – 5 kids, 2 AUdhd, 2 ASD – lone parent' ♥.

Sarah Davey, meanwhile, draws strength from, 'The relationship I have with my daughter and the mutual trust as she knows I will always do my best for her'.

Mindset

Your mindset is important! It is critical in supporting your loved one to the best of and beyond your ability.

Many describe a mindset as a set of beliefs that shape how you make sense of the world and yourself. It influences how you think, feel and behave in any given situation. This is not about well-being or being positive, it is simply about adapting to the challenges ahead. To use a buzzword, you need to develop a *growth mindset*, where you can get smarter and cannier by working at it. You need an adaptable mind. Always include humour in your approach as it helps when things get difficult.

Some people will criticise me for being blunt, but your journey will be filled with confrontation, 'what ifs' and crises, or boulders, as I call them. It is a journey that may be filled with anguish, grief, anger and, at times, endless despair. 'Strong words' you may say, but it is a journey that is very dependent on how you respond to the challenges you face. Your mindset determines how you respond and get the outcomes you want for you and your loved one.

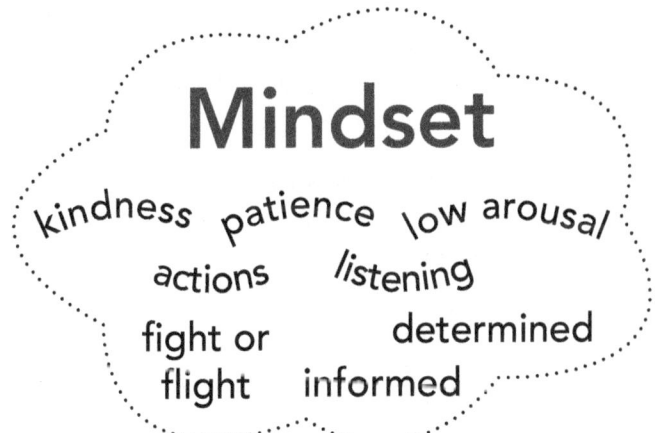

You may ask what should be in your growth mindset, and that is difficult to say without knowing you. Simply put, though, you need to be informed by *growing* your knowledge, to channel your frustrations to *grow* your determination, and take a low-arousal and listening approach to grow your kindness and patience. You also need to *grow* a good fight or flight response, so you know which battles to fight and which to abandon.

I have labelled my mindset as my 'Viking' hat. There are three aspects to my growth mindset: planning, mindfulness and being a warrior. Each part is interdependent. For example, when I need to confront people to gain access to services for Joe, I plan my campaign by reading up on statutory guidance and recent relevant research, and I am relentless in demanding access, like a warrior, and I am mindful not to get too emotional or personal.

Mindfulness ensures that I am in control of my responses to confrontation and supporting Joe through difficult moments.

Your kinder words should also be reflected in your actions. St David said that we should remember the little things. Ponder the meaning in his words and hopefully learn to link your kinder words with similar, kinder actions. Always remember that self-control rests with you. Never forget you need this mindset your whole life.

What if?

Some people may express feelings of grief or sorrow when they learn you have an autistic child and may wonder if you have similar feelings. However you feel, it may be hurtful to hear from people who try to empathise but may never fully understand. However you feel, it is important to remember that your feelings are valid, and it is quite normal to feel some grief for the child you have 'lost' (Bravo-Benítez *et al*, 2019).

This feeling is based on a 'what if' and assumes your child is going to develop perfectly and be another Einstein. No child comes with a manual and no child ever meets the development milestones perfectly. Don't forget that milestones are just a statistical measure to help determine progress rather than benchmark your child.

Some more unscrupulous people selling 'snake oil' therapy and 'cures' will take advantage of this grief. They will give you glossy brochures of smiling and happy children. What they are selling will never 'cure' your loved one. There is no 'cure' and there is only a long road.

You will come across people who will state that 'no one talks about the type of autism their loved one has', and you may feel this way too, sometimes. I know I do during Autism Awareness week when celebrity 'rocket scientists' and carers of loved ones with 'severe' autism fill my screen. However, some feel this way all the time, and they are very angry and depressed. They may feel as if they are victims, and many mourn their lost lives, from before they started living with autism. I understand how they feel, but I realised a long time ago that this mindset doesn't help anyone. It certainly doesn't help your loved one, and it stops you from having the best life your circumstances allow.

One of the most important things you will learn is how to handle 'what if?' scenarios, where there could be more than one outcome, or you wish to minimise the impact of an incident in the future. This is why you need to have an adaptable mindset that automatically adjusts to developing situations and develops mitigation strategies. I think of this as planning for the best while preparing for the worst.

For example, Joe uses the internet as his window onto the outside world. Any interruption of that access can be problematic for us. Over the years, I have ensured we have always had an alternative way to access the internet. Recently we upgraded to full-fibre broadband (my plan for the best) with a 5G backup dongle (my preparations for the worst).

Confrontation

My carer journey began a few years before the turn of the millennium and is filled with endless confrontation and battles with bureaucrats, gatekeepers and ignorant 'tut tuts'.

A gatekeeper is a person who you will meet at various services or other organisations who will 'triage' your situation and decide whether you can access their services. For example, a medical receptionist at your GP surgery or a DWP assessor are "gatekeepers". They in effect 'keep' the 'gate'... usually closed.

'Tut tuts' are those people who just don't get it, who share their opinion with you without asking, and just tut at you in their ignorance and indifference. Some 'tut tuts' will be armchair experts with a diploma in ignorance.

Confrontation comes from two sources: people and bureaucracy. Confrontation from people is caused by ignorance, malice and hate of difference. Confrontation with bureaucracy comes from statutory duties, policy, and budgets. Each of these requires you to remember that you are in control of how you respond, and that how you respond helps to determine the outcome. In all cases the law trumps policy.

Confrontation with people depends on your own personality and your mindset, as well as the fight, freeze or flight response. On your journey you will always encounter tut tuts and toxic people. There will always be people who need to ask what is 'wrong with your loved one?', and offer disciplinary or medical advice. Some will tell you to your face to think of others, that your loved one is a burden, and to think of the life you lost. We usually respond, if a response is warranted, with 'Not all ignorance is visible'. Humour and their embarrassment are your friends.

During a flight check-in we were once accused by a lady of pushing in front of her, despite being accompanied by a Special Assistance chap. My partner, in her best 'experienced teacher mode', turned to the lady and said', 'My dear, not all disabilities are visible, but your ignorance is plain to see'. We then carried on and left the lady with her embarrassment.

Some confrontations will be with 'shouty' and entitled people who are by their nature full of hate and malice. Toxic people will always be toxic, and they never respond to reason or logic. On our journey, we simply avoid these people as any confrontation can quickly escalate beyond your control and remember – not all harm is visible or immediate.

Your biggest source of confrontation, however, will be government agencies, whether local or national. Most people first encounter issues with their local government when they ask for support for their loved one in school. Similar issues can also arise when accessing physical and mental health services and applying for social security. There are usually numerous hoops and obstacles placed in your way. The best approach is to be firm and keeping asking why, and knowing the law. This is discussed elsewhere.

While you can't control people's bias or actions or change institutional policy, you can control your reaction. You have four choices when dealing with any conflict:

1. You can choose to respond in kind, which may escalate a confrontation. Ask yourself whether it is worth arguing with someone whose opinion you will never change.
2. You can choose not to respond by ignoring the challenge. Sometimes ignoring something can cause the other party to get more and more frustrated but does ensure you remain calm and in control.
3. You can try to defuse the situation. This probably only works when there is a crowd, or the other person has an open mind.
4. You can choose to walk away. This doesn't mean you lose but ensures you 'live' to fight another day.

These choices also apply when dealing with organisations. The people representing the organisations you deal with are not the organisation and they may choose to respond irrationally, because they are just people. Moreover, if you make matters personal, it may close pathways. That said, some people you deal with will make it personal, and some may do this deliberately to gatekeep you. During my journey, a local authority SEN officer once described us as 'pushy' parents (using friendlier words). Our response was calm and simply reminded the officer of her statutory duty and our duty to our loved one. We were of course quietly seething.

Help the growth aspect of your mindset by keeping detailed records, always expect timely minutes, always follow up in writing, and remind people of your expectations and the statutory timescales. Records help you deal with professionals' empty promises and holding them to those unfilled promises.

Crises or boulders

One of the forgotten aspects of any caring journey is the crises that may occur. Crises can be caused by the mood of your loved one or the hoops and closed doors others put in your way. A closed door, for example, could be a triaged 'no' when you need to access mental health services.

At times, life may seem to be a never-ending rollercoaster, with crises following one after another. Your mindset is key when dealing with the rollercoaster, and only by being mindful and listening with patience and kindness can you ride through the rollercoaster's twists and turns and wait for calmer times to come.

Pause and think about any patterns of "autistic" behaviour you encounter. Sometimes the pattern will repeat unless you understand the trigger. Your mindset is key to discovering the trigger and providing a meaningful and permanent solution. Many years ago, Joe always felt sick when first attending his senior school. Some people would put this down to anxiety caused by change, but it was caused by not completing homework. In Joe's eleven-year-old mind homework was schoolwork and should be done in school. We spoke to the SENCo whose said that Joe's wasn't completing all of his homework, and together with a gentle conversation with Joe, we realised that the stress of homework was the issue. The solution was relatively simple; Joe used the school homework club and we engaged a private tutor.

Welfare

Many carers do not volunteer for the role, nor do they have a choice. It is a duty created by love. A choice implies options, and the only other option available to carers is abandonment. Caring is something we do even though it may significantly impact our own financial, mental and physical welfare. It is my task to care for Joe until the end of my days, even if that means I leave early.

At times you may feel like a little dog in a circus jumping through fire hoops as you deal with bureaucracy and the chores that dominate your life. Some chores may include sourcing medication, doing extra washing, attending frequent meetings about your loved one. Sometimes the distraction and importance of these extra chores force many people to give up full-time work and lose meaningful social contact with friends and family.

This loss of social contact, whether through work or with friends, can lead to isolation, loneliness and declining mental and physical health. Andrea Heywood describes this as:

> *'The long-term impact of being a carer is that, over time, your needs take second, third or fourth place, depending upon how many loved ones you are caring for. Over 30 years, I have found that in the respite moments, reading and music have been vital to reclaim a sense of self.'*

Some carers, me included, have delayed or declined important medical appointments to ensure the care for their loved one is not interrupted. Other people will expect you to drop everything to solve a problem for them. For example, a carer I know was attending a cardiologist appointment but had to cancel all the scheduled tests because his loved one's residential day centre had run out of clothes. The centre expected him to drop everything to solve the problem, despite the centre having a washing machine and tumble drier.

Many will see this journey as a financial burden. Many will see your loved one as a burden. Many journals discuss the financial cost of bringing up an autistic child and supporting an autistic adult. The estimates include lost work opportunities and the costs of providing pastoral and medical support to your loved one.

Obviously, on a personal level, finances can be tight even with the financial support from social security, which is limited. The intrusiveness and pettiness of the bureaucracy around social security and social care payments can be worrisome. Tighter finances can increase your stress and impact your health.

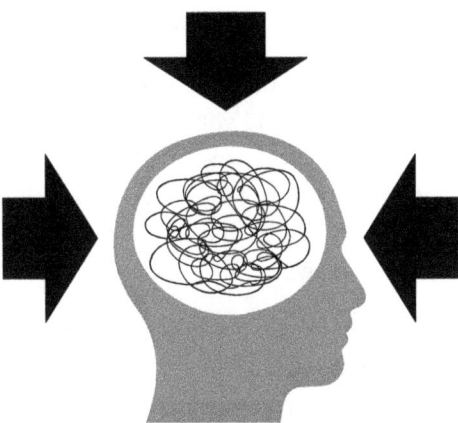

Recent scientific studies have compared the stress and exhaustion you may endure to that of a combat soldier on an active battlefield (Dixon, 2021). Holder (2010) also discusses this in detail. However, unlike soldiers, unpaid carers are not rotated out. Deb Wood describes caring as:

> *'Exhausting. Not just the caring side, the form filling, advocating, meetings, appointments, emails. They drain the life from me. My physical and MH have taken a battering. I had a stress-induced brain haemorrhage, struggle with my MH. No one understands the impact.'*

So, how do you deal with this almost-permanent fatigue and strain? It is easy for others to say you 'need to find time for you', while never comprehending what you do. However, it is important to remember the sentiment. Like a soldier, you spend a lot of time waiting. That could be time queuing in a shop, waiting at the GP surgery, waiting for the washing machine to finish etc. I call these moments 'snatched time'. It is these times I use to telephone friends, write this guide, and do many other things that are important to me. It is my time. Many carers forget about respite, where your loved one is cared for or supported by someone else. Respite can be helpful when you need some time to yourself.

There is a saying that 'a burden shared is a burden halved'. Soldiers learn to be part of a team, where some tasks are delegated, and others are shared. If you have a partner, learn to share the caring tasks. For example, my partner and I share the task of transporting Joe to and from his clubs and volunteering. If my wife takes him, I will usually collect him.

It is imperative, if you have a partner, that you talk to them frequently about how you feel about caring and your relationship together. There is some anecdotal evidence that a journey with autism can destroy relationships. Some internet sites suggest an 80% rate, but the reality is different. Harley *et al* (2010) suggest that the risk of divorce is about 24%, which is about twice the average.

Most of the carers I know, however, are in very stable relationships. This may sound simple, but make some alone time for you both, whether it is as simple as a walk to the shops or around your local park, or a quick coffee and cake in your local coffee shop. Time alone for you to be a couple is important. My wife and I try and do something at least once a week. I know it is easier said than done, but make use of any brief respite you may have to strengthen that relationship. We also make time for the other to do their own thing.

It is also helpful if you talk to others in your family or close friends about how you feel. Sharing might help you feel less alone. It certainly works for me when I talk to my father and brother. Sometimes, they see things from a different perspective which can help. That said, we usually talk about anything but caring, just so I can be myself momentarily.

Most areas have services and support networks for carers. Many of these are run by charities and may offer crafting courses and tea and chat meetups. Some will say, 'They don't want to hear more moaning carers', but others will find common ground and new friends who will understand and won't judge. Such groups have been very helpful to us. Marie Martin says, 'We all need to find our tribe' and Claire goes further and says the first words of advice they would give any carer is, 'Find a network of people with a life like yours: many can be online but some near you'.

Nationally, the bigger carer charities also provide online meetups and frequent courses like Pilates. As these meetups are always free, there is no harm trying them and the only thing you lose is time.

Elsewhere in this guide, I talk about the power of distraction as a strategy. Consider distracting yourself with a hobby, some volunteering, or just some trips that get you out and about. For example, I volunteer as a Parish Councillor and help with a mental health group in my local mental health trust. That time out helps me stay connected with the outside world.

One of the most important words many carers forget is NO. Prioritising your own needs is important, if only because if you neglect them, you may no longer be able to provide care. So, in the best interests of your loved one, you need to learn to say no.

Please also think of your loved one's siblings; they are also unpaid carers. Ensure they have considerable downtime and meaningful access to the support your local authority will provide.

So please understand this journey is not all doom and gloom. The following may be helpful:

- Make time for you, even if it is just snatched time.
- Look after your mental and physical health.
- Use respite care.
- Talk to your friends and family.
- Join a group or volunteer in your community.
- Work as a team.
- Celebrate every little victory and pebble.
- Be proud of the difference you make daily for your loved one.

One carer I have met on my journey, who wished to remain anonymous, summed it up perfectly:

> *'I'm sure there are but it's so hard to see them [friends and your partner alone] when you're stuck in a deep hole [from stress, doom & gloom]! I think being together 24/7 for a decade has made our bond stronger as a couple... I think the situation has also helped us to focus on the important things in life, I was never very materialistic, but I am even less so now. Happiness and love are what matters, if we can make each other smile or laugh then it's been a good day!'*

Personally, being a carer has done me good. I am a better person, in my opinion, because of my journey. Francesca L describes this far better than me:

> *'I believe my son(s) have made me a better parent and person. I have more understanding of difference and uniqueness and can celebrate it'.*

Milestones

A child's life is filled with developmental milestones and expectations, and this can be a focus of stress for many parents or carers. When you are on your second baby, you may realise that they are mainly loose guidelines rather than strict 'shoulds'. That said, some may be indicative of trouble ahead. If your doctor or district nurse isn't sympathetic, ask if they have lived experience. Medical practitioners with real lived experience will understand and answer your questions far better than those without.

Traditional milestones are still important. The moments when your loved one first speaks, crawls and walks are all precious and filled with joy. These are big boulder-sized milestones that hide the pebble-sized milestones. Pebble-sized milestones are simple things, like remembering a birthday, a little smile, a joke or answering the telephone. Most people celebrate the boulders and either ignore the pebbles or take them for granted.

On my journey, pebble-sized milestones are very significant and some are so small that they hide the enormous amount of work that it has taken to achieve them.

Recently, Joe graduated and wanted to attend the graduation ceremony. Some will say this is a big milestone, but it is supported by far more important pebbles in my opinion. Joe decided to get higher qualifications to increase his chances of finding meaningful work. That decision was a pebble. During the first year, Joe went by train on his own to college after several explorative journeys with his PA and us. This was a pebble. During the final year, Joe travelled to college by a DSA-funded taxi, another pebble. Every one of these pebbles made the huge smile on Joe's face on graduation day possible.

I can't tell you what pebbles will be important on your journey, but you will hopefully get lots of them that will prepare and support your loved one.

My list of dos

I have talked about my mindset, but I appreciate that not everyone will be comfortable developing and maintaining a robust frame of mind. Given that, I have distilled my approach into a list of 'dos'. This list is not exhaustive and is not in any order of importance. Take from it what works for you:

- Remember that you are the expert.
- Always ask why.
- Always 'stick it to the man'.
- Never accept 'no' as a final answer.
- Appeal every negative decision.
- Be sceptical.
- Be kind.
- Be patient.
- Ask for the Earth and you may get what you need.
- Know the law.
- Quote and use the law.
- Make notes and let them know you are making notes.
- Get everything promised in writing.
- Print important emails for future use.
- Record everything if you can (you are not being paranoid).
- Always expect the local government and health system to ignore you.
- Claim every benefit or discount because they won't tell you what you're missing out on.
- Claim every discount even if you think you are ineligible.
- Talk to other carers and parents, they will know the local wrinkles.
- The only people you can rely on are yourself and other carers.
- Learn to switch off everything but remain on standby.
- Understand your loved one's rights under the Mental Health Act (MHA).
- Understand your loved one's protected rights.

- Remember your other children.
- Be wary of people online.
- Remember you have rights.
- Learn to sleep whenever you can.
- Learn to have a few minutes for yourself.
- Remember unpaid carer's leave.
- Sleep, didn't I already mention that?

Who is the expert?

Many dictionaries describe being an expert along the lines of 'a person who is very knowledgeable about or skillful in a particular area'. Do you know who that describes?

You!

On this journey, you will learn to be the centre of knowledge of your loved one, a 'Jack of many trades', and an expert in many things most didn't even know existed. For example, you may know the names of every dinosaur because of your loved one's interest, and you will also know every section of the Autism Act, and your loved one's clinical needs better than any doctor… On my journey, I have also had to relearn areas of complex mathematics I'd forgotten about, and the stats of nearly every muscle car and piece of military hardware in the world.

Each little piece of information has kept me close to Joe and, like all knowledge, you never know when it will be useful. Once when we were on holiday, we noticed a mum struggling with her five-year-old who had an interest in dinosaurs. We struck up a holiday friendship centred around dinosaurs and autism. She suspected autism but was constantly fobbed off by family and professionals. Mum thought she was going 'nuts', but we reassured her that her instincts were correct.

Many professionals may expect you to defer to their 'superior' knowledge, without understanding that you probably know more than them because of your lived experience and the research you have done to understand and protect your loved one. You know how your loved one's version of autism presents and how other conditions interact. You know when your loved one is masking, has bad anxiety or is about to endure a meltdown or shutdown. Professionals who don't have lived experience of your loved one won't know any of this.

NHS clinical guidance classes you and your loved one as the experts and describes you as 'Experts by Experience'. There are good clinical reasons why they should listen. You may recall the tragic story of Oliver McGowan. There are quite a few similar stories.

I have only ever deferred to three professionals: two clinical psychologists with lived experience, and a senior school SENCO (special needs coordinator) running a department solely for autistic people. Each one has made a measurable and profound difference to my family and this journey. All the other professionals have had no choice but to listen.

Words of caution

One of the things I regret on this journey is not finding enough time to spend with my other children. Time with just them, without the intrusion of autism; time to just be with them, listen to them, laugh with them, support them, and appreciate their considerable achievements. Hindsight is wonderful, but please find or make the time because everything has consequences.

Some people will be critical of you no matter what you do. Try not to take it personally and, if possible, simply ignore them. Remember, most of them will never travel on this road and they will never understand. Moreover, they wouldn't last five minutes if they did.

You may notice that some friends and family drift away. It is their choice and probably you will be better for it anyway. Do not focus on the life you apparently lost; embrace the far richer world you now occupy.

Always be careful when using social media. Social media is a great source of information and friendship, but please exercise caution. People who you think 'get it' can turn instantly, and remember that no one is your friend unless you know them.

Follow genuine autistic people and carers; you will learn much from them. Avoid libertarians and people who claim to be autistic but aren't. You will learn to spot them. Some people can be very nasty and personal. It is not worth engaging with toxic people, because they will harm your well-being and you will never ever change their opinion. A tiny minority, I know as the 'thought police' and 'autism moms', will guarantee a pile-on with multitudes of criticism because of their large followings. They will say hurtful things about carers and autistic people with little regard for the impact on you, so be mindful. Some may accuse you of 'speaking over autistic people' or just call you 'allistic'. Please avoid them. If you post photos and videos of your loved one, expect some barbed comments. The block, mute and unfollow buttons are your friends.

With that said, please remember the people you encounter on this journey have feelings, and despite how they treat you and your loved one, always be mindful, and always respond with kindness. This shouldn't stop you from being assertive or critical, however. Those in positions of power may only be following procedures and policies of the organisations they represent. Please treat others as you'd like to be treated.

It is important to remember that you are a central and important part of the extended autistic community. Some may not appreciate your efforts, your plans, and the dreams you abandoned. As Paul Ridley often points out to me, '…it is society that exacts a huge toll on you rather than autism'.

As mentioned in my list of dos, one of the most precious things you need is sleep. You never get enough of it, but never to make decisions when you have had a broken night's sleep, and never scold your loved one for waking you up.

Anecdotally, many parents recognise that they have some autistic traits after a loved one is diagnosed, but it doesn't necessarily mean you are also autistic. Having a few traits will help you to understand your loved one better but may make dealing with officials a little more difficult. Some of these parents will discover that they are actually autistic.

Chapter 2:
About autism

'Autism' is a curious word to describe what this book is about. It was first used in 1908 by Eugen Bleuler to describe a schizophrenic patient. Bleuler derived the word from the Greek word *'autós'*, meaning self.

It is a simple word that can be controversial, scary, and empowering, depending on your point of view. It is something you can't hold. It is something that is both invisible and clearly visible. It can be disabling but also enabling.

Is autism an enigma? Hopefully, you already know the answer to that.

What is autism?

While this may sound like a simple question, it is a complex one that ultimately depends on your journey and point of view.

In Tongan, the word for autism is Takiwātanga, which translates to English as 'in their own time and space'. I think this defines it perfectly.

Autism is a lifelong developmental disability that affects how autistic people see, hear, and feel the world differently from other people. If you are autistic, you are autistic for life; autism is not an illness or disease and cannot be 'cured'. At times, it may appear that your loved one will have to pay rent on their right to exist. Often people feel being autistic is a fundamental aspect of their identity. A positive autistic identity is helpful in avoiding well-being or mental health issues (Davies et al, 2024).

Autism is essentially a different way of being in the world. Autism is applying logical responses when emotional responses are required. Most of the descriptions of autism are from the perspective of articulate and non-autistic professionals. In reality, this is comparing chalk with cheese. My favourite analogy is from the world of information technology: autism is the MacOS operating system and non-autism is the Windows operating system. Both operating systems do the same job in different ways. Most people prefer one and struggle with the other one. That struggle represents the perceived difficulties autistic people have. Simon, an autistic person I admire, explains it this way: 'I would say autism is the diagnosis much like Mac and Windows are the software… Neither is better.'

Some people claim autism is a 'fake' condition developed by psychiatrists to simply bundle commonly occurring conditions into a more accessible structure for them. These people are missing the point.

There are some quite shocking statistics surrounding the treatment of our loved ones (NAS, 2023). Thirty per cent fall into severe depression, they are eight times more likely to feel lonely, most have thoughts of suicide ideation, and there is a significantly increased risk of suicide in comparison with the general population. Many people say these statistics say more about society than your loved one.

Types of autism

There is an infinite variety of autism types, and you may well have heard the phrase, 'If you've met one autistic person, you've met one autistic person'. Despite this infinite variety, however, there are common traits that are used to classify autism.

Over the years there have been different flavours, or types, of autism, and in the future there are bound to be changes as society changes and our understanding evolves. Autism is defined in two documents: the International Classification of Diseases (ICD) from WHO; and the Diagnostic and Statistical Manual of Mental Health Disorders (DSM) from the American Psychiatric Association. The ICD is on revision 11 (although some countries still use version 10) and the DSM is at version 5 plus (commonly known as DSM V). The definition of autism will evolve as diagnostic criteria adjust to meet budgets, politics and societal understandings and pressure.

Previously, people were diagnosed with different named subtypes, like Asperger Syndrome, Classic Autism, Profound Autism, Kanner's Syndrome, Infantile Autism, PDA, Rett's Syndrome, Childhood Disintegrative Disorder (CDD) and Pervasive Developmental Disorder-Not Otherwise Specified (PDD-NOS). Presently there is only autism, split into numbered subtypes.

PDD-NOS is a 'mild' type of autism that presents a range of symptoms, but there may be insufficient traits to warrant to full autism diagnosis. (Because of the diagnostic criteria and thresholds rather than your loved one not being 'autistic enough'.)

Pathological Demand Avoidance (PDA) is controversial. The condition has common difficulties with autism but has an additional trait of exercising more control over everyday life. 'PDAers' have a need to control more of their lives to manage their anxiety. It can be very disabling.

Always remember: while there may be only one diagnostic autism (as defined in the diagnostic manuals), your loved one's version is unique, so embrace your particular flavour; ours is 'Jalapeno'.

Needs

The picture of autism is further complicated by adjectives added to subdivide autism based on apparent need. These words include 'mild', 'profound' and 'severe'. Such adjectives are supposed to convey the severity of the symptoms and the support need required. However, this assumes that needs are constant and similar, but the needs of a person with severe autism and a learning disability are totally different to someone with Asperger's. That doesn't mean that the person with Asperger's has fewer needs or needs less support. In contrast, the needs and support required are fundamentally different and are not comparable. To compare them is disingenuous and may be dangerous.

The professionals

Professionals classify autism as a series of deficits from some perceived norm. Every few years their official description of autism changes to reflect new diagnostic criteria. Many autistic people prefer to talk about the positives rather than these deficits.

The Center for Disease Control (CDC) in the US describes autism as 'a developmental disability caused by differences in the brain'. The UK National Autism Society (NAS) also describes autism in terms of deficits. Both organisations' descriptions centre on the perceived problems that autistic people experience. They cite issues with social communication and interaction, restricted or repetitive behaviours or interests and sensitivity. They also mention different ways of learning, moving, and paying attention. It is important to note that non-autistic people may also have some of these traits. These characteristics may make life very challenging.

Some of the deficits described by professionals include:

- Failure to make and maintain eye contact.
- Ordering objects.
- Changes of routine and prescribed routines.
- Stimming – 'involuntary' movements like hand flapping.
- Obsessive interests or highly focused interests.
- Echolalia – repeating words and phrases.
- Lack of imagination.
- Social communication issues and social interaction issues.

- Repetitive behaviour and restricted behaviour.
- Over- and under-sensitivity.
- Extreme anxiety, meltdowns and shutdowns.

Autistic people have difficulties with interpreting both verbal and non-verbal language like gestures or tone of voice. Some autistic people are unable to speak or have limited speech and may be described as non-verbal, while other autistic people have very good language skills but struggle to understand sarcasm or tone of voice. Other challenges include seeing the world in black and white, or not understanding 'abstract' concepts, needing extra processing time, and repeating what others have said. Most of these need to be looked at in the context of non-autistic people's behaviour, especially when they are characterised as deficits. Autistic people just do these 'normal' human behaviours in greater detail and depth.

Let's look at eye contact as an example. Many non-autistic people expect a certain amount of eye contact from a person they are speaking to, and may see the avoidance of such eye contact as a sign of 'shiftiness', or that the person is lying or hiding something. Indeed, 'Look at me when I'm talking to you!' is a common demand that parents might make of their children. And yet many non-autistic people only make fleeting eye contact themselves, and others complain if you make too much eye contact, which can come across as aggressive or threatening. These social expectations and unspoken and nuanced rules often make little sense to people with autism and are hard for them to follow, especially given that many experience eye contact as painful or deeply uncomfortable – as if they are looking into someone's soul. Avoiding eye contact is, for many autistic people, therefore simply a way of avoiding discomfort or being overwhelmed by information, and this can actually improve their ability to listen to the words being spoken – my favourite autistic person describes this as the 'freckle count conundrum': you either get a freckle count by insisting they look at you, or they actually listen to you. You can't have both.

Chapter 2: About autism

Ordering objects and rigidly following strict routines are common behaviours of autistic people, which may seem a little bizarre until you consider that, if a non-autistic adult did the same, you would simply say they were organised. Everyone has routines or rituals. Think about how you prepare breakfast or how you plan and structure your day, and your reaction if someone breaks that routine or you have to change your plans at the last minute. Think also about the rituals we all have – the sequences in which we dress, wash or brush our teeth, the order in which we make our cups of tea (milk first or last?), arranging collections, like stamps or coins, or counting things in our environment for no reason.

Many autism therapies focus on repetitive or 'involuntary' body movements, like hand flapping. Self-stimulation or stimming is important for autistic people. Non-autistic people also stim by twirling their hair, tapping a mouse, drumming, clicking their fingers or bouncing their foot from a crossed knee. Some non-autistic people stick their tongues out when they are concentrating.

Obsessive interests are also common among non-autistic people – they are simply called hobbies. If a non-autistic person has a detailed knowledge of a subject or spends a lot of time collecting particular objects, they are described as dedicated or classed as an expert. What is the difference? Please note, many autistic people prefer to describe their hobbies as special interests.

Many professionals think autistic people are rigid or lacking imagination, and many cite a lack of empathy. Imagination is simply thinking, looking at something from a different perspective and acting on it. Have you ever seen an autistic child playing with Lego? One of my heroes is Alan Turing; I wonder if he'd be classed as lacking imagination?

One of the core parts of autism is the sensory issues people with autism often face, but these are no different to the sensory issues many non-autistic people have. Think what you do on a bright sunny day; you wear sunglasses. Think how irritable you are when you have a cold, or how loud the world appears when you are hungover.

An autistic perspective

Many autistic people say that autism is a sensory processing difference, and that at its core it is this that affects how people perceive the world and interact with others. Autistic people see, hear, taste and feel the world differently to non-autistic folk.

Many autistic people see the world more brightly than the majority. It is not that there is more light, it is just that everything is far more vivid. Reds are deep and that Day-Glo orange can be as painful as looking directly at the sun. If you get migraines, you may understand this aspect.

Sound is complicated, and many autistic people have heightened hearing and are sensitive to certain frequencies. For example, Joe can hear our ultrasonic cat scarer and is sensitive to the noise vacuum cleaners make. Noise-cancelling headphones, iPods and earmuffs or ear defenders are essential when travelling by air.

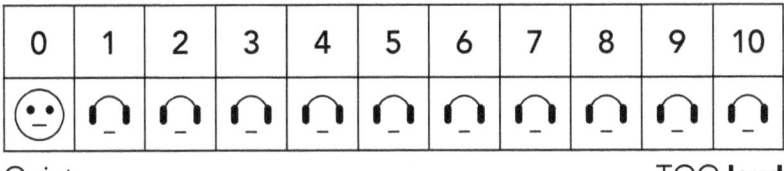

Quiet   TOO **loud**

Taste, smell and texture are important when talking about food and drink. Think about Marmite and you may understand how intense these things can be.

Texture is also important when considering clothing. You know that shudder you get when 'someone walks through your soul', or that little speck of grit in your shoe that feels like a mountain? Well, imagine that shudder coupled with every fibre of your clothing being like that speck of grit.

What carers think

Whether you class yourself as a carer or a parent, you will understand autism and its consequences.

It may seem strange, but I know about the 'deficits', the social awkwardness with non-autistic people, the logical and black-and-white view of the world, the robust social-justice outlook, the vulnerability, and every diagnosis and all the other issues, but I only see Joe.

For me, autism is simply a logical and robust view of reality using clear glasses, and occasionally binoculars. An autistic person is just a person with the gain on every sense turned up above the manufacturer's maximum or below the manufacturer's minimum.

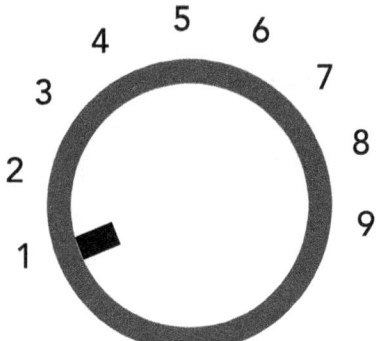

Communication is a two-way street and social communication deficits exist on both sides. If you think about the confrontation that can occur between non-autistic people because of communication mistakes, ask where the communication deficit actually lies. Joe goes to various social clubs for autistic people, and it is a joy to see the stress-free and non-awkward communication that takes place.

When I asked other carers how they saw their journey, many said how tough it can be. Claire explained that it is

> 'tough in its own right and should be acknowledged more: caring for your disabled offspring can be Groundhog Day'.

'SPuzzling' explains where the distress originates:

> 'For me autism & LD haven't been the issue, battling the services is what caused me the distress...'

When talking about autism, most carers describe it in the same enlightened fashion. 'D' described autism as, 'Exceptionally and truly beautiful intellect with no educational setting suitable to embrace and nurture. My son's view: "My Autism is a variety of strengths and weaknesses. My neurons are wired differently, and my perspective is different in seeing between and beyond".'

Kate Alton explained that,

> 'From watching my kid, Autism is feeling the world so deeply, and yet not always knowing what to do with those feelings; loving people, but not having the innate, untaught social understanding about how to connect; being amazing, yet constantly anxious about being misunderstood'.

'SPuzzling' went on to explain that, '...if more people thought like my son the world would be a better place'.

A carer's journey with autism may vary but each carer does the utmost to ensure the best outcome. 'The Tattered Fox' describes their journey as: 'Walking through the individual maze that we are, to find the one spark that works for that person'.

Susan Phelps explains how 'There are things people with autism can do really well, but thinking, "if they can do that, they should be able to do this," isn't true. You have to meet them where they are. They do grow and learn, but it's rarely linear.'

Bundles

Autism rarely occurs on its own and it is usually bundled with something else like dyspraxia or ADHD. Only about four per cent of autistic people do not have a bundle. Each bundle is unique, and the dynamics of each bundle are subject to change. Some bundles are comorbid, and others are co-occurring, meaning that they simply co-exist in the same person but aren't necessarily related. For example, ADHD is comorbid, but diabetes is co-occurring.

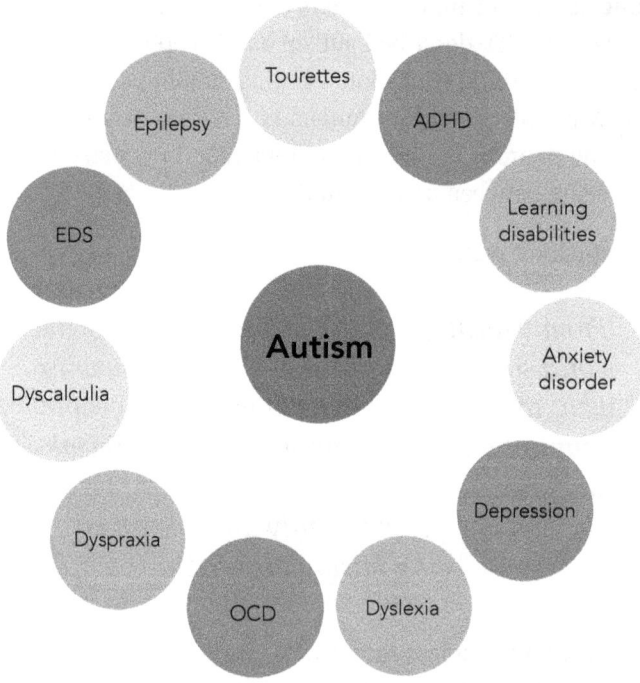

It is reported in scientific journals that some 50-70% of autistic people may have ADHD, (Hours *et al*, 2022). Some autistic/ADHD people report a race condition (where one condition contradicts the other) between the impulsiveness of ADHD and the restraint of autism. Sometimes this race makes life difficult.

Jon Adams (@soundcube) explains:

> 'My head doesn't cope well with being a 24/7 referee wondering who's going to kick off next and cause an "inconsistency".'

Many people have been able to quieten the 'race condition' with appropriate ADHD medication or appropriate support.

Anxiety is one of the core parts of any bundle, and between 40-60% of autistic people have heightened anxiety. This anxiety is unlike anything you have felt, and you really need to listen if your loved one has more anxiety than usual. Anxiety can lead to depression – the pit of despair and the pit of no return. An autistic gentleman (Simon) once said, 'Autistic people don't fake anxiety, they fake being okay'.

Catatonia is relatively common in autistic people, with research suggesting that nearly 20% of autistic people also have this condition. Catatonia can be difficult to diagnose due to overlaps with behaviours like stimming. Sometimes it is very observable with increased slowness, lethargy, increased mutism, and some stupor. The usual treatments appear to be ineffective.

Bipolar disorder (BPD) is a psychiatric condition. People with bipolar disorder have both extreme emotional highs (mania) and extreme emotional lows (depression). Some people later diagnosed with autism were first diagnosed with BPD before it later being revised to autism by an experienced clinician. Anecdotally, autistic women are more likely to be misdiagnosed in this way.

Many autistic people may develop depression because of the way society treats them. Symptoms can be severe. Therapies used for non-autistic people may not work for autistic people unless the therapist is appropriately trained and is able to tune the therapy to the specific needs of the autistic person.

Dyslexia and dyscalculia can be quite disabling and can undermine a person's self-esteem considerably. Both can be worked around, but without appropriate intervention, they can impact someone's education and life chances. Given that both are as complex as autism, it is advisable to seek advice.

Bundles make autism very complicated, especially when some professionals ignore such possibilities and make diagnosis complicated. It is one of the reasons carers are so important and need to be included in every conversation. For ethical and confidential reasons, you need to exclude yourself from some conversations, like those your loved one has with a mental health therapist, but obviously included in safeguarding and way forward conversations.

Many of these conditions have a common root. Many genetic studies point to a common cause and a significant number of autistic people meet the criteria for an ADHD diagnosis. Interestingly, siblings of autistic people run twice the 'risk' of having autism, while the risk for ADHD when a sibling has ADHD is six times higher than the general population. Moreover, a Swedish study found that members of the extended family of an autistic person are more likely to have ADHD (Rusting, 2018).

Autism is not a mental illness, but autistic people are more likely to develop a mental illness. A recent study (Ribolsi, 2022) estimated that approximately 35% of autistic people may have a psychosis. Moreover, over 60% of schizophrenia sufferers may have autistic traits. This can make supporting an autistic person with comorbid conditions complex.

There are some conditions that may appear to some to be autism, OCD or ADHD. Paediatric Acute-onset Neuropsychiatric Disorders, or PANS, is one such condition, however PANS is caused by an infection and can be cured with appropriate medication.

Social rules

Non-autistic people have hidden social rules and rituals based on minute body language cues, changes in tone, posture, and social and other hierarchies. Many of these hidden cues and rules are either missed by autistic people or seen as irrelevant to progress. This etiquette is at the core of the difficulties autistic people face. In effect, social rules cause autism.

For example, let's consider the 'Hello, how are you?' handshake or ritual greeting that many non-autistic people find important when meeting or greeting someone they don't know, whether face to face or by telephone. There is an expectation that the responder will simply say, 'Thank you, I'm fine', or an equivalent. Effectively, each non-autistic person is disinterested in the well-being of the other person. If you greet an autistic person this way, however, you may get a flat 'fine' if they have been 'trained' to respond 'correctly', but you are just as likely to get a detailed account of their day. I once asked an autistic chap I knew how he was and got an in-depth description of how his anti-psychotic drugs were making him feel.

Most autistic people are open, honest, direct and factual, with no reading between the lines. Non-autistic people may see this as rude, abrasive or blunt, which can cause confrontation because of those hidden rules that centre around what you mustn't or shouldn't say. If a non-autistic person was from Yorkshire, most people would accept the directness...

> A story from my journey involves queuing in a supermarket behind a lady buying several large boxes of jam doughnuts. Joe, then six years old, suggested that the lady should make an alternative purchase because doughnuts are very fattening. The lady overheard and was quite offended that a six-year-old was policing her shopping. Thinking logically, Joe was probably correct. My partner enjoyed taking Joe shopping with her because of his unfiltered honesty when she tried on clothes. Sadly, he adapted and learnt to say what was expected.

These rules are relaxed for people society thinks as exceptional, usually the very wealthy and entitled, however, exceptions are never extended to disabled people. The economist Harriet Taylor Mill once said: 'No society in which eccentricity is a matter of reproach, can be in a wholesome state'.

Terminology explained

There are a lot of unfamiliar words and concepts associated with autism. Many of them need context to understand. Some of these terms have different meanings to those you may be used to.

The spectrum

This is probably a hard concept to grasp given the words chosen, and many people assume that it is some sort of linear, rainbow scale where some people are more autistic than others.

This assumption is incorrect, and each colour represents a real autistic trait, like red represents social communication and indigo represents echolalia, for example. This misconception is reinforced by phrases like 'we are all a little autistic' and 'on the spectrum'.

Chapter 2: About autism

Professionals describe it as a spectrum of deficits rather than a spectrum of abilities. Many autistic people prefer the abilities approach.

The company IDR Labs has a succinct and meaningful way to represent the autistic spectrum and it may help many overcome this misconception. The company depicts the spectrum as a pie chart with equally sized slices for each trait. Each slice is coloured to the degree the trait is present in that person. Some traits and the interaction between comorbidities are not represented, but hopefully their representation will help.

Some people have a concept that this translates into a 'spikey' profile.

Every autistic person is affected to some degree by several of these traits. If your loved one only ticks one or two of these traits, they may not be classed as autistic. For example, if they have issues with social communication, they will probably be diagnosed with a social communication disorder. Autism is a bundle of many related symptoms and experiences grouped together that make things simpler to hold and understand. Imagine how complex life would be if every autistic person had six or seven separate and distinct diagnoses?

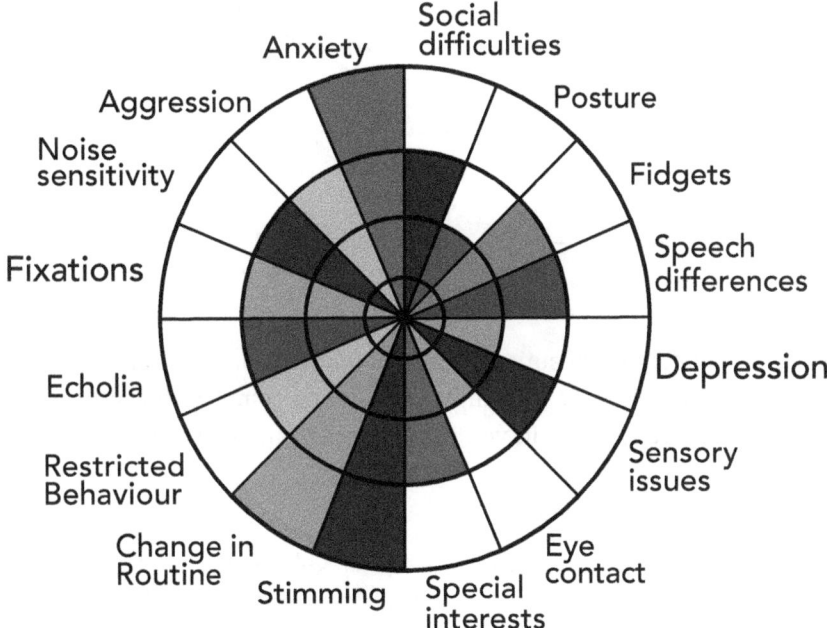

You may have heard that some people suggest that most young people spend too much time of using devices, and it may lead to something called "virtual autism". Virtual autism is used to describe the social isolation, behavioural issues, and inadequate emotional growth that some children appear to have. If someone suggests that this is why your loved one is different, please take what they say with a large pinch of salt. As you know your loved one's use of devices enables their development and growth whilst providing a safe place and a means of communication.

Abstract concepts

Abstract concepts is thinking about things that are not concrete. This is part of the diagnostic criteria for a learning disability. For example, some people may not get sarcasm. Some professionals think that this also applies to autistic people. As a consequence, one of the stereotypes that surrounds autism is that autistic people are incapable of abstract thinking.

On my journey, every autistic person I have met has understood many complex and abstract things better than me. Some also can distil the most abstract concepts into simple choices. Joe is an example of this.

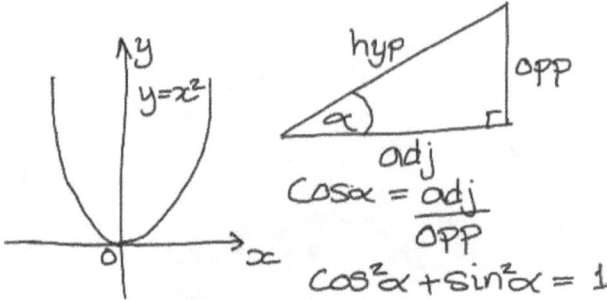

One of the stereotypes of autistic people is that they are good at mathematics, which is an inherently abstract and complex subject. So, if you think logically about it, you should understand that this deficit is probably nonsense.

> As an example, when Joe was studying A-level mathematics, he used to coach younger autistic people in his 'Base' at school. (A base is a safe place only autistic students can enter.) The mathematics teachers had failed to explain some abstract concepts to these students, but Joe was able to. This raises the question of who has the abstract concept deficit; teachers, or students?

Special interests

The term 'special interests' relates to the intense interests and in-depth knowledge many autistic people have, often in very specific subjects. Non-autistic people with in-depth knowledge or skill are considered experts.

Special interests are apparently one of the key features of autism, but it's worth asking if someone had a more mainstream interest like cars, computer games or music, would this still be considered a 'special interest' and an indicator that they may be autistic?

Most people have hobbies and interests that they are passionate about, and this is a great way to connect with like-minded communities. It is important to remember that being autistic is more than just 'having a hyper-hobby', but if your loved one does have one, embrace it!

These hobbies evolve with time and in some cases can form the start of careers. They also provide predictability and help with managing the unpredictability of daily life. They could be said to act as anchors for many people. In many cases, they also provide a vehicle for socialising. For example, if someone is fanatical about a football team, they can socialise more easily with people who follow the same team. On my journey, I have learnt about dinosaurs, Pokémon, and muscle cars.

Some autistic children like to dismantle things because of their special interest in understanding how things work. For those of you whose loved one has such an interest, a great source of free objects is Freegle or Freecycle, the recycling and reuse organisation. Most towns have branches.

See also Monotropism (p.57).

Perception, literalism and logic

As you know, autistic people perceive the world very differently from non-autistic people; the world is literal and filled with patterns. This perception is at the heart of autism. There is a saying about dreamers viewing the world through rose-coloured glasses... Well, in contrast, autistic people see the world through polarised binoculars; they notice the things you don't and only black and white factual reality.

My world is literal, there is no reading between the lines, only factual reality. This may take some adjustment on your part, but with time you may come to embrace it. Some will label you and your loved one as shy, lacking confidence, rude, insensitive etc, but ignore them. You will develop a way of thinking literally automatically.

Non-autistic people who speak and think this way are lauded, especially if they are successful. Moreover, just think of the lovely people from Yorkshire and you will get this aspect of autism.

The DWP has provided a lovely example to illustrate this. You may know that Universal Credit has an online journal where people log their job hunting and changes in circumstances. A section of the journal has a page dedicated to personal details. To avoid anxiety, we deal with the DWP, but leave Joe to deal with the journal. The journal uses two-factor authentication via a mobile phone. The journal only provides a single box for a phone number, and, importantly, the box is labelled as mobile. For the two-factor authentication, this is Joe's number. Despite our home (landline) number being in the journal notes, the DWP generally telephones Joe against guidance. To solve this problem, the DWP say we should put our landline number in the mobile box. That is an issue for Joe because it is labelled 'mobile'. Their suggestion will also break the two-factor identification as our landline is an old-fashioned telephone. A simple solution would be for the DWP to have an *alternative* telephone box.

Shutdown/meltdown

A meltdown or shutdown is a consequence of reaching a crisis point caused by high levels of stress or anxiety. The person is simply overwhelmed and loses control of their behaviour. Every person has a different threshold before they tip into a crisis.

Both meltdowns and shutdowns are temporary states, but they can take a while to recover from. Remember, the person hasn't flipped and has not suddenly become mentally ill or unstable. It is just one of those days and even non-autistic folk have them.

A meltdown is the visible and audible consequence of reaching that crisis point. A meltdown is not a tantrum or a sulk and shouldn't be described as such. A person reaching this point is in despair. They may be vocal, cry uncontrollably, lash out physically or verbally, or they might even self-harm. A meltdown is like a fight or flight response.

A shutdown is a less visible and silent consequence of reaching that same crisis point, with the person literally shutting down. They may become selectively mute, appear almost catatonic and may choose to isolate themselves. A person may be lethargic, may lose the ability to move and be less functionally skilled. Irritability may also increase. A shutdown is like a freeze response.

Responding to a meltdown or shutdown is very person centred. What works for one may not work for another. The best thing you can do is to remain calm and patient. It may be necessary to help the person to a quieter and safer place or simply give them some space, but only do so with their consent. Don't badger them if they are not responding, as many executive functions will have gone offline. Sometimes just physically being there is enough.

Anticipating when your loved one is being overwhelmed takes time and experience. Your loved one will also learn to anticipate and may eventually be able to self-regulate this aspect of autism. It requires patience and observation. For example, Joe occasionally leaves family gatherings by going for a walk or retreating to a quieter part of the house. A while ago, Joe was chastised by a relative for leaving a wedding reception. A sibling intervened before the relative made a shutdown inevitable. After a short walk, Joe later returned to the reception refreshed.

A few autistic people have described a shutdown as, 'Like a car idling that is at full throttle at the same time', 'When you hit a PC key so many times the whole system locks up', and 'Like I'm stuck inside my head. Can't move, can't speak. When I get to a certain level of distress it's like parts of my brain are shutting down. It's not in my control at all.'

Simon explained that:

> *'Meltdowns differ from person to person but from my experience it's like a panic attack but rather than brought on by anxiety or stress, it is caused by sensory overload or sheer mental exhaustion. Everything, including my own thoughts, is too much, painful, and incomprehensible'.*

As a family, we use the DEFCON warning system to indicate our proximity to shut down and meltdown. We try to stay around 4 and 5. If we near 3 we quietly ask questions, and at DEFCON 2 our attention is fully focused on supporting our loved one.

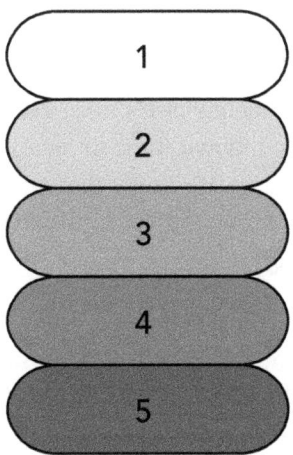

Masking

Masking (or camouflaging) is the ultimate form of acting. It comes at a great personal cost. Autistic people try to adapt to fit into a socially expected form, or a perceived mould required by other people. Autistic people may mimic the behaviour of those around them, like copying non-verbal behaviours and developing complex social scripts to get by when they need to be social. Like someone at a Venetian masked ball, they wear a mask to hide their inner self.

For example, at work, an autistic person may be very quiet and just get on with their work but will go to the communal kitchen every few hours like everyone else. At work, they may suppress their desire to stim or to listen to music, or they may contribute to a conversation in order to fit in when they would really prefer to remain silent.

Masking is a protective process to avoid the prejudice and judgement that comes from being seen as different. Most autistic people will have considerable experience of judgemental prejudice from extended family members, teachers and their peers. This prejudice may have taken the form of being the butt of someone else's joke, exclusion, bullying and assault. Autistic people need 'down' time to recover from masking. Anna Rebowska, a psychiatrist, says, 'We know that masking and camouflaging are major risk factors for suicide and yet continue with interventions that actively teach and encourage it'.

Simon described masking as like being:

> '...on stage in a one-person play, trying to be someone else for other people's benefit'.

Another anonymous autistic person described it as:

> *'Pretending to be someone you're not in order to avoid unwanted attention that leads to a sense of hostility and fear resulting in acute anxiety'.*

Whatever form a person's masking takes, or whatever it is masking, it always involves a lot of internal suppression and control.

Masking can also include code-switching, where someone adjusts to meet the cultural expectations of an environment or an organisation. Code-switching involves adjusting your style of speech, appearance, behaviour and expression in ways to boost the comfort of others. This adds another layer of complexity for autistic people in work and education.

Stimming

Stimming, or self-stimulation, is an important part of being autistic. Stimming is any repetitive or unusual movement or noise, such as finger clicking, pacing, laughing, rocking etc. Each person will have their own unique range of stims, or movements. Stims seem to help some autistic people manage emotions and cope with overwhelming situations, and it can therefore be thought of as a coping mechanism to deal with fear, anger, anxiety and excitement. Stimming also helps with the huge processing tasks and unwinding from social contact or being outside of a comfort zone. Some stims are caused by environmental factors and it may be possible to reduce or stop them by changing the environment.

Stimming is a form of self-distraction and produces a calming effect, with the whole person focused on the stim rather than the 'stressor'. The physical immediacy distracts the brain from the anxiety, and helps avoid a four F response (Fight, Flight, Freeze, or Fawn). Even non-autistic people do this. Stimming also helps when someone appears under sensitive by stimulating their underactive senses.

Some stimming may be harmful or self-injurious, such as head banging or self-cutting. Obviously, if your loved one has harmful stims, then it's important seek appropriate help and support.

Particular stims and their frequency are very good indicators of stress, while others are indicative of contentment. For example, hand flapping away from your loved one's body may indicate contentment while flapping close to your loved one's body may indicate heightened anxiety. With time, you will learn what means what.

Stimming should be thought of as a pressure release valve, like on steam engine. The more coal that is fed to the fire, the more the steam pressure builds, until the engine catastrophically fails. The pressure release valve, like stimming, avoids this by letting the pressure out slowly and preventing it from building up.

Some stims will irritate you and others, and because of society's invisible and incoherent rules there are places where stimming should be discouraged to minimise confrontation. However, suppressing stims is a form of masking (see above), and it can be challenging for a person to do this for any length of time.

Try not to chastise your loved one for stimming. Instead, help them evolve their stimming to be less irritating. Totally shutting down stimming guarantees a meltdown or shutdown. Ensure your loved one has a safe place for them to be themselves with their stims.

Some people class stimming as 'behaviours' and they will describe some behaviours as errant. They may not understand the importance of stimming and may insist on 'quiet hands' in the classroom, for example. Policies like this are dangerous as they ignore the stress/pressure release and processing parts of stimming. Ask yourself whether it is better to have some tolerance to ensure everyone, especially those undiagnosed, have some release?

Some people will recommend therapies to remove the stim from your loved one. If you encounter such a behaviourist, ask why you should go down this path, and be careful as some evidence-based therapies may cause PTSD.

There are therefore three important things to consider with stimming: that it is an important method of self-regulation, that is a useful safety valve, and that it is something that everyone does, including non-autistic people.

The self-regulation aspect has been described to me as a 'metronome for your body', 'How we express the gyrations of our mind physically' and 'Self-soothing when feeling anxious'.

The safety valve aspect has been described as follows: 'If emotions are water, stimming is like the steam coming from a kettle if you were to hold down the button for too long'.

Finally, as stated, we all stim, autistic or not. Think about how little children suck their thumbs, or how you may fiddle with a pen in a boring meeting, and others pace when they are anxious. Some people bite their nails when they are nervous, tap their feet or jiggle their leg, and others play with their hair or fidget.

Burnout

Modern life can be very stressful, and this is even more so for autistic people. Burnout can occur as a result of navigating a world built for non-autistic people and living up to the expectations and demands that society throws at people. Burnout is a consequence of excessive masking.

Burnout describes the point where stress has turned to distress and manifests as despair. Its main symptoms are pervasive and long-term mental, emotional and physical exhaustion linked to a collapse in tolerance of most stimuli. Burnout can seriously impact someone's mental health. A loss of skills is to be expected and, for example, someone with strong verbal abilities could find themselves unable to talk.

It can occur at any time, but particularly during major transitions, such as puberty, leaving senior school etc. It can be coupled with a collapse in self-worth, direction, and a worry that it could become permanent. There is a danger of increased suicide ideation. Many autistic people remove themselves temporarily to preserve what's left of themselves.

Recovery can be delayed by a lack of empathy from non-autistic people who can sometimes struggle to understand. We all have a need for duvet days, but this is a duvet day on steroids that can last for weeks and months.

Simon describes burnout as being like an:

> *'Empty battery leading to temporary CPU shutdown, all systems on standby until cooling is complete'.*

Another autistic (anonymous) person said:

> *'I'm tired. Which also means I'm tired of having to explain myself to people who aren't even interested in listening.'*

Executive functioning

Executive functioning refers to a person's ability to process and organise information. It is a fuzzy concept but includes organising, planning, remembering, paying attention, controlling responses, and responding to life. It is something many people do automatically, while others develop strategies to manage this important life skill.

Around 80% of autistic people have issues with executive functioning[1]. I have worked with rocket scientists who can solve the most complex engineering problems imaginable, but have considerable difficulty with life.

My favourite autistic person explained this as picking the appropriate spark plugs for your car rather than just any spark plugs.

Everybody, whether autistic or not, shows differences in their executive function. You may know some people who pay attention to minor details but can never see the bigger picture. Others can see the bigger picture but can never focus on the details. Some forget it is the little things that make everything work.

Some people have issues with maintaining attention, but also hyper-focus on special interests. Attention and focus are different and, with support, the skill of paying attention can be developed. You may recall that the most remarkable scientist ever had attention issues in school – many know this singular chap simply as Albert.

All this said, though, executive functioning issues can make life considerably more difficult for many people. It can cause intense frustration. It can affect day-to-day organisation, like remembering a doctor's appointment, remembering to pre-book a train ticket, or paying for something on time.

My favourite autistic person describes their executive function as:

> 'A deep brain fog between what you need to do and what you are doing'.

An anonymous autistic person describes theirs as:

> 'Paralysis of the mind', and that they get 'so overwhelmed it minimises normal body and mind functions. Simple tasks like eating, personal hygiene and sleeping become challenging as [I am] physically shutdown.'

---

1 See: adultautismcenter.org/blog/autism-and-executive-function; leicspart.nhs.uk/autism-space/health-and-lifestyle/autism-and-executive-functioning-skills/

It is possible to work around the issues executive functioning in some cases. For example I use my iPhone calendar to remind me to periodically contact the people that matter to me.

> When Joe used to travel by train to college, he used a weekly electronic ticket, so he wouldn't ever forget to take his ticket with him. (It also helped to avoid people). Joe was always reminded on Sunday evening to buy a ticket for the following week.

Anxiety

Many autistic people have heightened anxiety. Some also have a diagnosis of an anxiety disorder. Heightened anxiety can be very problematic and without management or strategies to deal with it, it can lead to a loss of sleep, loss of self-esteem and self-harm. In extreme circumstances, it can result in suicidal ideation. Anxiety experienced by autistic people is nothing like the butterflies you may experience when you do something new, go to an interview or stand close to the edge of a cliff. This is several orders of magnitude more: it envelopes every fibre of your being. Anxiety is that little critical voice that constantly and toxically whispers in your ear in the quiet of the night. The voice that ensures the consequences become circular and feed on each other creating a 'doom-loop', a sort of virtual Groundhog Day in your mind. Breaking that loop is sometimes very difficult.

According to the NAS (2023), 94% of autistic people have anxiety and 30% have severe depression (medical definition). Most have had their lives severely impacted by anxiety and a significant number have depression as a result. Anxiety can therefore be dangerous, and its management is paramount to ensure you and your loved one have a reasonable life.

This is one of the more complex areas of supporting an autistic person. Their environment, the number of people around them, their current mood, or an event or something that was recently said can seriously affect someone's anxiety. Such situations can be dynamic and require some knowledge of the autistic person.

On this journey, humour and distraction can help, but they only kick the can down the road until the cause of the anxiety is known or resolved.

An anonymous autistic person described anxiety as:

> *'Trying to do something whilst wading neck high in setting concrete so you can't move, breathe, or do what you would really (deep down) like to do'.*

Kev Brown described autistic anxiety as:

> *'Like walking through a glass wall knowing it is going to hurt, but staying where you are will hurt you more'.*

From my and other carers perspectives, anxiety appears as a constant feeling that something will go catastrophically wrong. The consequences are distress and near-constant worry.

Neurodivergence and neurodiversity

Neurodivergence describes every human that is not 'typical', and applies to all such atypical people, including people with autism, ADHD, dyslexia etc. This term excludes your average Joe. Non-divergent people are known as neurotypical, or NTs.

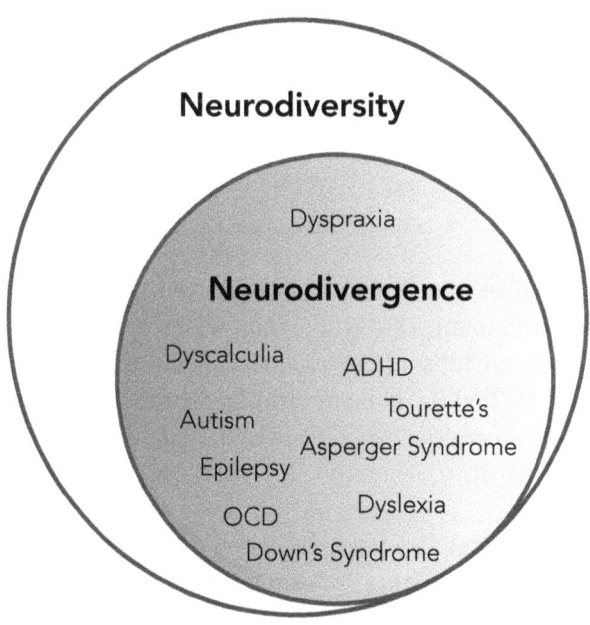

Neurodiversity, on the other hand, describes every human that exists. Every human has a unique brain with a different spiky profile to everyone else. This includes non-autistic people, autistic people, dyslexic people...

There is a complicated debate surrounding both of these terms and their usage. Both terms appear to have different meanings to different communities. For example, many businesses and institutions support neurodiversity and have signed up to be 'Disability Confident Employers' with HM Government and the DWP. Registered companies may display a logo on their paperwork and websites. Sadly, some of the registered companies have taken a tokenistic approach, whilst others have embraced the concept and offer jobs through companies like Auticon and "Ambitious for Autism". This is reflected in the recent Buckland Review which stated that "Autistic graduates are twice as likely to be unemployed after 15 months as non-disabled graduates".

Other groups may claim the term 'neurodivergence' as theirs to reflect their unique nature. Both terms are connected by claimed identity, rights and benefits. For example, many autistic people see autism as part of their identity. A detailed discussion of the issues surrounding both words can be found in Jones *et al* (2024).

Hyperlexia

Some autistic people have remarkable talents, and a common one of these is being able to read proficiently from a very early age. Up to 20% of autistic people may have this ability. However, it doesn't mean that typical social communication is better than expected.

Edward Phillips explains how he read *Silmarillion* by JRR Tolkien at the age of nine: 'Silmarillion at age 9... yeah he's "normal" – sheesh.'

Monotropism

Monotropism describes autistic special interests and the intense focus that is often associated with them. The term monotropism was developed by Dinah Murray et al to explain autism from an autistic point of view (Murray, 2020). Many autistic people find the monotropism theory of autism to be more consistent with their personal experiences than other theories of autism.

Apraxia

Some people with autism also have childhood apraxia of speech, a neurological disorder that makes spoken language extremely difficult. But most non-verbal individuals on the autism spectrum don't have apraxia; they just don't speak. Apraxia is caused by poor motor control of the tongue, jaw and mouth, making speech very difficult.

Apraxia is usually diagnosed after ruling out other conditions. There is currently no test for apraxia. It is usually diagnosed by speech and language specialists.

Selective mutism

Selective mutism is an anxiety disorder in which a person loses the ability to speak in some circumstances. Usually, speech is lost when the individual is stressed, or it is triggered by a person, location or a topic of conversation, for example. Triggers are unique to each person, and it needs to be remembered that the phenomenon is *involuntary*.

Many people may misunderstand selective mutism and may think the individual is simply being awkward or obstructive. This issue causes confusion and difficulty, and some assume indifference or arrogance. However, the contrary is true and the 'frozen' person cares and would always want to join the conversation, but simply can't. This should not be confused with shyness.

Beck Stack explains:

> *'Anxiety is so high I'm literally rendered speechless. Trapped in a world of silence. I have no control, like a deer caught in the headlights. Frozen in fear. It's debilitating.'*

An autistic person reminded me that *selective* mutism is *situational* mutism because it better describes how it affects most people. Another described it as a brain freeze that limits their mouth from forming words. This is one of the reasons why many autistic people don't like using the telephone – more on this in a moment.

Many autistic people report disbelief and hostility in others when they become situationally mute. Others can't understand its involuntary nature and generally make absurd accusations.

Caroline explained:

> *'I would get shouted at for not replying when I just can't. I'm not being rude, but I am stopping a meltdown. And I usually have to leave which some people have said is disrespectful.'*

One of the assumptions people make is that everyone can talk on the telephone. Obviously, this assumption has consequences for people who are selectively mute. There may be moments during a conversation when there are periods of silence because of the mutism. If a phone conversation has a period of silence, what do you assume? Disinterest, a dropped call, a zone out? Most people would respond by hanging up, but can you imagine how frustrating this can be for the mute person?

Some mental health services operate out-of-hours telephone services to provide immediate support to people who are desperate. If someone is selectively mute or non-verbal, how would that work? Could this assumption prove fatal in some of these cases?

I have been working with my local Mental Health Trust to encourage them to have a text or WhatsApp option for non-verbal and selectively mute people. The Samaritans already offer such a service.

When being asked about mutism, Helen, an autistic person, ironically responded, 'Um, well, you've put me on the spot. I'll get back to you in three days when I've processed your question.'

For many autistic people, mutism is very difficult. Amanda explains that 'It's like being locked inside yourself', while Sophie Porritt adds that it's 'A bit like temporary locked-in syndrome in my brain'. Rebecca Coles succinctly explains that it is a result of, 'As sensory overload and overwhelm'.

William Rice explains the overwhelm many endure as:

> *'Being so completely overwhelmed by a situation that, although every part of you is screaming for you to say something, you simply can't. For me, it feels like an overload followed by a shutdown.'*

Obviously, the inability to speak endures while the trigger is still present. Some describe this as analogous to an invasion. 'The Tolerant Dinosaur' explains that this aspect, '…feels like an internal invasion of an external threat. Once that threat is established, it takes all of your focus to try to drive it back out, which typically can't happen until the external threat is removed.'

Echolalia

Echolalia is described as the unsolicited repetition of sounds made by another person. It is called palilalia if a person repeats something they have said themself. This can be an automatic or a delayed response. While it can be very irritating, always pause before responding as the person may be unable to control the behaviour.

If your loved one repeats what you say, think of it as making sure they heard you correctly and giving themselves thinking space. If your loved one repeats the same saying, think of it as a stim. Everyone does this to some extent – think about the songs that you sometimes find yourself singing after it has been played on the radio, how politicians and others give themselves thinking time, how you respond when someone gives you a new address or telephone number.

One anonymous autistic person describes it as '...feeling like a living, breathing LP with a scratch in it'.

Alexithymia

Alexithymia is described as a person being unable to identify and characterise their own emotions, or those of others. It can be perceived as a lack of empathy because the person's responses may be inappropriate. A significant percentage (around 10%) of the total population have this (Wang *et al*, 2022).

If we think about this differently for a moment and link it to those invisible societal rules and subtle body language that your loved one misses or doesn't know about, is it any wonder their responses may be not what's expected? Also, you may have noticed your loved one's facial expressions may not match their current feeling. Here, an angry grimace can mean many things including profound happiness, and remember: you don't have to be smiling to be happy and content.

Everyone gets this wrong. People misinterpret others' facial expressions or tone of voice all the time. Consider also how strangers respond to you when you are in emotional or physical pain... they don't, if they can't see the pain.

A few years ago, there was a TV series called 'The Transporters'. The series was designed to help autistic children understand and identify emotions. It was very helpful to us as a family. It is still available on YouTube.

Things to be aware of

As mentioned earlier, there is a common saying that 'If you met one autistic person you've met one autistic person'. Like everyone else, every autistic person is unique. There are many traits that are shared in varying degrees by most autistic people. You could think of this section as 'autism consequences 101' – that is things you should be aware of because they may carry consequences for your autistic loved one and you.

Eye contact

We have already touched on eye contact, but this is a big one. Many autistic people find it difficult to make or maintain eye contact. Sadly, many non-autistic people interpret this as a sign of social or personal indifference or a lack of interest, or that it indicates that the person is not trustworthy or is lying. Obviously, this has consequences in a school environment and, more importantly, in a justice setting. In a school setting it can lead to a bullied autistic child being sanctioned rather than the bully (there is considerable anecdotal evidence of this). In a justice setting it can make an accused appear guilty when they may be innocent or it can undermine the testimony of an autistic victim or witness.

It appears that many autistic people are over-stimulated by eye contact and as a result it is stressful and uncomfortable. Brain scans show that the pain is an actual felt experience.

Many people expect others to look at them when they are talking. Teachers sometimes insist on this and ask children to 'Look at me when I am talking'. Many forget that most people don't listen with their eyes, and a simple solution to this is to say instead, 'Listen to me while I am talking'.

One autistic person explained that:

> 'The eyes are windows to the soul, and I don't want creepers peering in my windows'.

Kyle Morgan explains that:

> 'Another person's day will not be affected in the slightest if I avoid eye contact while talking to them. I am avoiding severe discomfort, nearly PAIN, by not making eye contact. The other person would barely notice, and move on... I won't have to have a meltdown later.'

Is it worth challenging the concept that autistic people need to get better at eye contact or is it an example of non-autistic people wanting autistic people to present like they do?

Sensory overload

Most people accept that migraines are more than nuclear-powered headaches. Most accept the pain is overwhelming and a sufferer will need time to recover. Most people accept that there is a huge sensory component to a migraine that is overwhelming. Autistic sensory overload is equivalent to this, or even considerably worse.

Generally, most people can automatically tune out unimportant sensory stimuli so they can respond to new stimuli. For example, a clock ticking loudly or the whir of an electric fan. However, many autistic people are unable to do this and, as a result, they may be overwhelmed as they try to make sense of everything. Zeliadt (2019) describes this in detail.

To help you understand, recall the last time you were desperate to sleep on a warm summer night but couldn't. All you heard and felt was the traffic, the clock ticking, the whir of the fan, the lump in your pillow... It appeared that everything was conspiring to stop you from sleeping. If you focus on the desperation and the feeling of overwhelm, you may start to understand. Joe once described a nosebleed as 'drowning in his own blood'.

An illustrative but often-overlooked sensory issue is temperature, which many autistic people are sensitive to, as well to changes in temperature. Consider how you feel when it is a hot, muggy summer day. You probably know some non-autistic people are sensitive to high and low temperatures, but as you may have realised by now, autistic people do things so much better. The consequences for autistic people can be profound and temperature-based triggers can quickly escalate out of control, leading to burnout, meltdown, and shutdown.

Here are some quotes from autistic people describing the effect of temperature:

> *'I feel sticky and sweaty. My skin is itchy and irritated. It's easier to get in a bad mood. I get dizzy, my blood pressure drops. I do not like it AT ALL.'*

> *'It's like someone taking out my batteries. The moment it gets cooler or breezier, I snap back. I don't mind the heat per se, it's the muggy airless heat.'*

Meanwhile, an anonymous carer explained that:

> *'I keep a constant eye on our daughter. She knows when she's hot but struggles to recognise when she overheats, and it comes out as an anxiety attack. We have a fan right by her in the day, keep window ajar at night for breeze, cold drinks, keep an eye on her fluid intake...'*

Joe is particularly sensitive to temperature and changes in temperature. To avoid the consequences, we installed A/C in our bedrooms.

Food and eating disorders

Many autistic people have a difficult relationship with food. For example, some prefer 'beige' food, others will only have a specific list of certain foods they can eat, and some have sensory issues. Some develop issues because of the circumstances in which they first encountered a particular food and how they were feeling at that particular moment. For example, an autistic friend of mine won't eat smoked salmon, because they associate it with a memory of when they felt they were letting someone down. Others could have a similar experience with a new or existing food that becomes associated with a painful memory. For example, when Joe was a toddler, he had tonsillitis and the only food that was not painful for him was milk, grapes and spaghetti. As a family, we only ate spaghetti for years after this, but slowly, thanks to Heinz Ketchup, we expanded the diet. Today Joe eats most things. A parent sums up the consequences of this succinctly: '..."new improved flavour", the absolute horror'.

It's therefore important never to make food a battle or to make adverse comments about your loved one's shape etc. Unfortunately, manufacturers and shops often don't help us by tweaking recipes or discontinuing lines.

An eating disorder is usually described as a mental health condition, where people use food to cope with emotions and stressful situations. Eating disorders affect both sexes, and research suggests that up to 25% of those with an eating disorder may be autistic.

The most common types of eating disorders include:

- Anorexia nervosa, a condition of not eating enough, probably exercising too much, or a combination of both.
- Bulimia a binge-eating condition associated with being sick, taking laxatives or exercising too much to prevent weight gain.
- Binge-eating disorder is where a lot of food is eaten over a short period.
- ARFID (avoidant and restrictive food intake disorder) is where someone has a limited diet in terms of range and quantity. AFRID is often caused by sensory differences.

The links between eating disorders and autism are poorly understood, but they tend to be longer lasting and more severe than in the general population. It must be remembered that eating disorders have the highest mortality rates of any mental illness, and, moreover, the longer a person has an eating disorder the harder it is to recover.

The prevalence of eating disorders in autistic people is complex but can involve sensory issues around the smell, taste and texture of some foods, an already restricted diet, comfort patterns and predictability and control. There is some correlation with those with heightened alexithymia traits being more susceptible.

A young autistic woman I know developed an eating disorder following a school's refusal to make a reasonable adjustment by allowing her to eat lunch somewhere other than the school canteen. The smell and noise of the canteen were a trigger for her and eventually led to school refusal. The young lady was hospitalised as a consequence of her school failing to do their statutory duty.

If your loved one develops eating issues, please seek urgent help as you don't want to endure what this family is enduring.

Sleep

What has sleep got to do with autism you may ask? If you are confused, please be thankful.

Sleep issues affect around 30% of the general population. Many autistic people (50-80%) can often have trouble sleeping, whether falling asleep or staying asleep. The reasons are complex but include trouble with relaxing or winding down and irregular melatonin levels. It is disruptive for siblings, parents and carers, and this issue affects autistic children and adults.

The following may contribute to poor sleep:

- Being unsettled
- Not having enough melatonin
- Anxiety

- Epilepsy
- Blue light from phones or other devices
- Sensory issues
- Food allergies
- Hypersomnia

Many of the reasons are common to most people, but as you have probably learnt by now, autism takes everything to the next level. Moreover, some may suffer from 'pavor nocturnus', or night terrors. Jon Adams explains, 'I've had nightmares since a child – always liked the quiet when everyone went to bed – still the same 55 years later'.

Anxiety always appears worse at night when that little critter can whisper nasty things into your loved one's ear. With no distractions, anxiety can have a field day as different scenarios play in endless loops increasing the anxiety and brain activity.

A lack of sleep can make certain parts of the condition more prominent. Just like you, autistic people can appear more irrational and irritable after little or no sleep, and some autistic traits like repetitive behaviours can be more pronounced. A lack of sleep may be indicative of depression. Better sleep won't cure autism, but it will lessen the symptoms, and for you carers, better sleep will enable you to cope and support your loved one better. Failing that, there is always coffee.

We have learnt distraction helps break this cycle. When Joe disturbs me because of an anxiety loop, I listen rationally, explain, and reassure. Joe then watches some cartoons while eating breakfast cereal. Laughter also breaks the loop for Joe. To help him get back to sleep, Joe takes a few Kalms, a herbal sleep remedy. This approach works 90% of the time.

If a lack of melatonin is suspected, please speak to a qualified clinician before going down this road. This approach doesn't always work. Jill Jablonski explains: 'My 18-year-old struggles to sleep due to anxiety and OCD. She takes melatonin to help. She is constantly tired, she zones out whilst getting ready for bed which can end up taking hours.'

In contrast Leanne reports that melatonin made no difference to her loved one, but drowsy antihistamine did.

Some autistic people prefer the night when there are fewer sensory issues.

Sarah, an autistic adult explains:

> *'I find nights hard. I would work better with naps in the day when I am actually tired (mid-morning, mid-afternoon) which I think is triggered by sensory overload. Night is so hard as my brain calms.'*

A good sleep routine can help and familiar sounds like relaxing music, white noise, the shipping forecast etc may also help. It is perfectly fine to keep your teddy bears and similar toys into adulthood and it is perfectly fine to take them on holidays (remember they need a passport ☺). The familiarity and constant smell can help when sleeping in an unfamiliar location. Some studies suggest incorporating some light reading into the bedtime routine may also help.

You may need to persevere with a new regimen for several nights before you will really know if it works for your loved one, and remember to seek medical advice if sleeping is a persistent issue.

It is assumed that your loved one's bedroom is only for sleep. There are no TVs or PCs in Joe's bedroom; this is by design to remove temptation. Luckily, Joe has a separate room for his PC and TV.

Non-verbal autism

This section provides a basic overview of non-verbal autism. This trait is not listed in the diagnostic criteria. Many are diagnosed with type 3 or 'severe' autism. Some non-verbal people will develop some speech. Some make sounds that have meaning to those who know them.

Many non-verbal autistic people may also have a learning disability. Some don't speak because of apraxia, a neurological speaking disorder addressed earlier. Some non-verbal people choose not to speak.

The diagnosis of non-verbal autism is complicated by the difficulty in distinguishing between children who have no spoken language (non-verbal), younger children who have not yet developed verbal language (pre-verbal), or non-communicative children. The presence of some echolalic speech is a significant predictor for the acquisition of spoken language.

Despite their difficulties, non-verbal people can make considerable contributions to society. For example, the best-selling book, *The Reason I Jump*, was written by Naoki Higashida, a non-verbal Japanese gentleman.

Technology has provided many non-verbal people with a means of communicating with the outside world. Find out what works for your loved one and speak with a speech and language therapist. Remember, 'PECS' may be appropriate, which stands for picture exchange communication system. People using PECS are taught to take a picture of a desired item in exchange for that item or need. The handing over of the picture starts a "conversation". PECS is said to work well at home and classroom.

Interoception

Interoception governs how your body interprets important signals, for example when you are hungry, cold etc. Most people believe that you only have five senses, but your body has another three: vestibular, proprioception and interoception. Interoception is how you feel inside your body. Think of it as that feeling in your tummy, for example, when you get a brown envelope through your letter box or when you're nervous about something. Interoception can affect self-regulation, intuition, self-awareness and social understanding.

Usually, if you are in discomfort, you do something to change or remove the cause. For example, many of us have had a 'rock' in a shoe and it has usually been a tiny spec and we usually respond by removing it. For many autistic people, that 'rock' feeling is probably felt for a particle smaller than dust. In this example, the discomfort could grow and become a blister.

Anger rumination

Anger rumination is a cognitive-emotional process linked to a tendency to dwell on frustrating experiences and recall past anger experiences. Remembering past incidents can exhaust self-regulation and cause the person to get 'stuck'. Being stuck leads to preservation. It can be a catch-22.

Inappropriate behaviour

A lot of play for autistic children is classed as *inappropriate*. Apparently, it isn't how you are supposed to play, as if there is some manual on the subject. Some see inappropriate play as showing a lack of imagination and an inability to project reality onto play. Some people use these perceived issues as early indicators of autism. It is as if your loved one is being criticised for being a child.

The classic inappropriate behaviour is lining up toy cars. Joe did this to some extent and knew every car by model and colour etc. As an adult, you get criticised if you don't line up your cars between silly white lines. Moreover, as a family you will be familiar with the traffic jam, so lining up cars does demonstrate an ability to project reality into play. The irony is probably lost on many.

Some schools have behaviour policies and primary schools have a 'quiet hands' policy and carpet time where all the children sit on a carpet in front of a teacher. 'Quiet hands' classifies hand flapping, fidget toys and fidgeting as errant or inappropriate behaviour because it is apparently distracting. However, the non-autistic person who finds it distracting often doesn't appreciate the benefit it brings. Those promoting these policies usually claim that the rules have to be the same for everyone, or everyone will want to be an exception. You may recall, however, that the law talks about reasonable adjustments and protected traits, and a request for some leeway for your autistic child should be taken seriously.

Obviously, some ways of play or use of language are indicative of autism, but never forget every child plays differently and always remember to play *with* your children.

Early death

The government is acutely aware that autistic people die much earlier than their peers. The latest autism strategy and NHS Long Term Plans reflect this fact.

The reasons for poorer health outcomes for autistic people include:

- They may not recognise or act on early symptoms of an illness (lumps, bumps, recurring pain etc) and may only seek help when very ill.
- They may struggle to comply with treatments.
- They lack of support to access healthcare, because of choosing to live alone or with no family.
- Healthcare is not responsive to their needs.

An often-overlooked phenomenon but very relevant when accessing medical advice is that autistic people feel pain differently to non-autistic folk; some may feel less pain, and some will feel excruciating pain. I cover this in greater detail elsewhere, but if a professional is unaware that autistic people feel pain differently, the recommended treatment may be inappropriate.

Many medical professionals have no lived experience, and their medical training will usually only focus on non-autistic people. If your loved one says they are in pain, take it seriously and always follow the precautionary principle to act, and never hesitate. I can only illustrate this point with the story of a friend of mine who had recurring 'mild' headaches and his GP kept dismissing him. Luckily, on his final visit to the GP he saw a locum who knew what was wrong because he had lived experience. My friend had a type 4/5 brain tumour. He was in his 30s when he passed, but that locum gave him five extra years.

A recent systematic review paper (Newell, 2023) on suicide and autism reported that the ideation of suicide among autistic people was 34%, those with actual suicide plans 22%, those who attempted suicide was around 25%, and mental health issues were reported in 80% of autistic people. The reasons surrounding suicide are complex, but succinctly come down to how autistic people are treated by society. The background rate of suicide (non-autistic people) is about 0.01%.

Suicide is probably the greatest cause of early death among younger autistic people, and the collateral damage of each death is huge. Family and friends will wonder what else they could have done. The guilt and grief apparently never subside, and this also affects those who managed to save their loved ones. On my journey, I know three mums affected by this guilt, and I will share two of their stories.

Several years ago, a young autistic gentleman was supported by a local authority. The gentleman was 'estranged' from his parents and lived in a little privately rented flat with some support from the LA. At some point in the story, it was decided he was coping, and the support was allegedly reduced. Later, he received a negative DWP letter. Bailiffs found his body in a cupboard; he had been dead for nine months. His parents tried frequently to have some well-being information (is he happy and coping?) from the local authority without success.[2]

Another story I heard involves an autistic teenager. The teenager's best friend moved out of the area and the impact on this young lady was huge. Her parents were terrified to leave her alone. For years they tried to access mental health services, and always got the same feeble lip service and excuses. One night, after another attempted suicide, her mother 'abandoned' her daughter in A&E. Faced with no choice, the authorities sectioned the young lady and provided the help that was desperately needed. The family still provide most of the support to their daughter.[3]

These stories haunt me, and not just because I know some of the people involved, and I strive to ensure Joe has the support needed to avoid these consequences, but sadly my time here is finite and the constant need for vigilance is draining.

One of the many things people say after someone has died by suicide is 'If only we knew'. Many mental health trusts operate Suicide Prevention (SPA) schemes accessed by telephone and offer Crisis Cafes. However, they may be inaccessible to autistic people; there is an assumption that everyone can use the telephone, but as discussed, that is not the case for all autistic people who may be situationally mute or non-verbal.

Something most people forget is that most people who are depressed pretend to be happy. Think back to those invisible social rules, and your feigned interest in everyone else. Please make time to listen to your loved one. Make a point of contacting them constantly and consistently if they live elsewhere. Understand the collateral consequences of such a death.

Sometimes when an autistic person has tried to take their life, medics make empty promises about follow-up support. It is a recurring theme for many autistic people.

---

2   Daily Mail Online article, 17 September 2019
3   Personal correspondence.

Abbey describes her journey:

> *'441 days ago I was admitted to A&E following a suicide attempt. 441 days ago I was told I would see the crisis team. 441 days ago I was told I would receive a referral for counselling. 441 days ago I was told I would receive info about mental health services – still nothing'.*

On our journey, when we were worried, we *harassed* the medics and authorities to get support for Joe. If you are faced with a similar hole, please harass them as a Viking would.

Change

This is a big thing and will probably be one of the aspects of autism that will make your life interesting. Change can trigger the deepest of responses and the darkest of emotions. You may find dealing with the consequences of change frustrating. When you think about change and the consequences of change, you may realise that it is not change itself but the uncertainty and the fear of the unexpected that is at the core of this issue. There is also the expectation that everything will always be the same. Many carers simply give up and keep everything the same.

Simon explains these consequences as:

> *'A computer freezing and not working no matter what button I press. Will need to turn it off and turn it on again.'* Another anonymous autistic person explained change and its consequences as being *'Like a bomb went off'*.

Change, especially unexpected change, can be very distressing. It can be something as simple as a broken plate or a nosebleed in the night. Responding to change or the absence of routine is unique to everyone. Expected and creeping change may be easier, especially if it is discussed openly. For example, Joe's favourite Great Aunt deteriorated over several months before her expected passing in hospital. He coped the best out of all of us. He chose to remember her as she was the last Christmas she spent with us.

There are two theories that help you to understand the complexity of change. One is the 'intense world theory', which suggests that autistic people focus on details rather than the whole picture. Another theory, 'disorder of prediction', suggests autistic people struggle to see the future, and this trait can make the world frighteningly random.

Many things that most families take for granted, like a trip out to a restaurant for example, require military planning and manoeuvres to reduce the consequences. Emma, a carer I respect, explains that a simple trip to a restaurant starts as an idea expressed a week before, to a possibility on day six, to a firm commitment on day five, to addressing worries about a menu change on day four, to reassuring that everything will be the same on day three… On the actual day, leaving the house follows a schedule, the same table in the restaurant…

Change can cover things as simple as new clothes. Some autistic people always buy the same clothes, others always wash new clothes, and others may prefer to borrow a sibling's or parent's clothes. This may be simply down to comfort and the subconscious effort to minimise discomfort that can increase anxiety.

Change can therefore be very subtle, including things most people wouldn't even notice, like tiny changes in packaging. An anonymous carer explained this: 'Yes Birds Eye burgers "now with added plant protein", sigh. He's never touched a Jaffa Cake since they changed the letter J on the box.'

Change can also cover running out of things, like herbal sleep remedies. I always get these in bulk (and pray they will never be discontinued).

Simon explained change as follows:

> 'Autistic brains don't have the same tracks, so any changes need new signs, signals and destinations'. He went on to say, 'Some change can lead to refusal. If you pause and think about why change is difficult, think how you feel when you meet someone new, how you may wonder what they will think of you, will they like you, will conversation be easy or stilted etc. Autistic people think all of these things simultaneously and that obviously requires a lot of processing.'

We take an informed approach to change; we discuss what will happen, what unexpected things may happen, and what we have already done to mitigate the consequences. We also include Joe in big decisions. For example, when we had to buy a 'new' family car, Joe and I visited numerous car showrooms to narrow the choice. During this time, Joe studied the safety records of every potential choice. I am not saying that had any influence, but we now have a Volvo.

As a family, we 'plan for the best but prepare for the worst', as I have said. This single phrase sums up how we manage change, especially unexpected change. Unexpected change can lead to meltdown, shutdown, self-harm, heightened anxiety and behavioural changes. Unexpected change is stressful and may be momentarily harmful. At these times, your loved one may be aggressive or withdrawn, as if someone has thrown a personality change switch. Preparing is necessary to mitigate the expected anxiety and sometimes profound consequences of change. Social stories may be a great help with this.

Most unexpected changes can in fact be expected. For example, power cuts happen, and it is possible to plan for them. We have several large USB power banks, wind-up and rechargeable camping lanterns and torches and a wind-up radio. However, this is not always enough.

Many years ago, I bought an uninterruptible power supply (UPS) for my PC to ensure I could work during outages and to protect my PC from brownouts. Most significant devices used by Joe are now on UPSs we adapted after some consequences. Our broadband router and associated networking equipment are also on a UPS. Joe's TV and Amazon Fire TV device are on a UPS.

Internet access is important to Joe; it provides information, supports a podcasting special interest, and offers him a window to the outside world. Over the years we have had extra data on our mobile phones to provide momentary hot spots, but your loved one borrowing your phone is not always convenient. More recently we invested in a pay-as-you-go Mifi device. The added benefit of this is you can take your broadband with you whenever you travel.

We also manage change by building redundancies into our approach to life. This can mean doubling up on favourites, having two of everything or an alternative.

Alternatives can't always be used, but a simple example is that I have two mobiles, each on a different network, and my partner is on a different network again. This means there is always an alternative means of contacting us.

As a family, we also double up on devices (only when we can afford to) or we keep a replaced device for that autistic rainy day. Old laptops and PCs are prime examples of this. We also ensure content is replicated across devices. For example, if your loved one loves story tapes or audiobooks and certain genres of music, replicate that content across all your devices.

Several years ago, Joe jumped into a swimming pool with his iPod in a pocket of his trunks. Luckily, Joe's mum had an identical iPod with the same content. The expectant anxiety was avoided because we had a prepared solution. That iPod is still in use today.

When Joe was little, certain clothes were his favourites. We quickly learnt to always buy the next size up. This indulgence reduced the impact of change when a favourite jumper no longer fitted.

I asked some autistic people how they describe change and how it affects them – I hope you find their colourful explanations helpful:

> 'Change for me, is like taking a completed thousand piece jigsaw, throwing it in the air, then trying to cope, with the immense psychological, emotional and physical pain, of a new picture.'
>
> – William Rice.

> 'Imagine a ship. Ships are big and don't like to turn and take a long time to speed up and slow down. Non-Autistic people are small ships, Autistic people are REALLY big forking ships... and they are a lot easier to crash. Gotta take it carefully.'
>
> – Edward Phillips

> 'For me as an autistic person change feels like bereavement.'
>
> – 'Autjoy'

And here are some descriptions of change from anonymous autistic contributors:

> 'Change is at first my worst nightmare. If I'm able to stim right away I can sort through my chaotic emotions and make some logical decisions about the change I'm facing. Once I'm calmer I can then decide how this change actually affects me and if the distress was worth it.'

> 'Change means slow down, risks up. Danger up. The less people see it the more stressful it is.'

> '...being left in a foreign country without a map.'

Change, especially very unexpected change, can alter behaviour. Many autistic people have very strong social-justice traits and may seek to punish themselves if they believe they are the cause of some misfortune. For example, a car crash will knock most people's confidence, but it may cause an autistic person to question whether they should be allowed to drive, and some may even think of ripping up their licences.

Sometimes people use different words, like 'transition', to camouflage profound change. You transition from childhood to being an adult. You transition from primary school to secondary school. These examples can be particularly difficult for autistic people. So, on your journey, don't camouflage, downplay or underestimate the nature of the change, because honesty is best, and it enables you and your loved one to plan for and work through the change for better outcomes.

Change is also difficult for others, even non-autistic people, when they see it as an inconvenience or a threat to their power or position. UK law has the concept of a reasonable adjustment, which means that others are expected to accommodate the needs of vulnerable and disabled people. Many professional people often think of their own convenience rather than making minor changes, and they behave in a rather stereotypically autistic way. This is best illustrated by a story about a friend's non-verbal autistic loved one, known as Bob for the sake of this story.

Bob, who also has a profound learning disability, had to be admitted to a burns unit following an incident at a day centre. He doesn't like medical staff or unexpected changes and relies on his carers to cope with the world. Bob's hospital stay was difficult for everyone, and especially for medical professionals who refused to change their ways to accommodate his needs. After discharge, Bob had to return to the hospital for a follow-up appointment to confirm he was healing and there was no residual infection. The round trip to the hospital took three hours, and Bob's carers have to rely on special taxis because of his needs. Bob's carers plan everything down to the smallest detail to accommodate his needs. They kept in touch with staff, they said when they would arrive for the booked appointment, they reminded staff of Bob's needs and likely responses. Bob's carers asked that someone meet them in case Bob refused to get out of the taxi, or he had a meltdown or 'did a runner'. When they arrived at the hospital, Bob refused to leave the taxi and his agitation quickly rose to DEFCON 1. Bob's carers phoned the staff and asked if someone would come down to meet them, as previously arranged. The staff refused as they were busy, it was inconvenient etc. It was a 100m walk from the ward to the taxi. The staff would not budge. Bob, meanwhile, had passed the point of no return; his personal Armageddon had arrived. Bob's carers telephoned the ward to say that they had to take Bob home or the consequences and recovery would be weeks long. About halfway home the hospital phoned to say they could see Bob if they could bring him to the ward.

All of this was preventable by a simple walk to a taxi. A simple and very reasonable adjustment. Some people have rigid thinking and professionals are not immune to this trait. It could be argued that their experience or presumed superior knowledge underpins that rigidity. This rigidity makes change difficult for them. While I have no advice to give on this, I have always asked to speak to a more senior person to get a second opinion. Whether this approach makes a difference really depends on the culture of the people and organisation you are dealing with.

In the case of Bob, it made no difference when he was at the hospital, but when my friend returned to the hospital with photographs of Bob's healing wounds it did. A registrar demanded Bob's carers bring him back to the hospital for another assessment by the registrar. My friend asked for another opinion and the senior consultant overruled the registrar because he had seen how Bob behaved when he was in hospital.

Refusal

Refusal is complicated and the reasons for it are many. There are two types of refusal: autistic refusal and refusal by others to make reasonable adjustments.

Autistic refusal at the simplest level is an avoidance of situations that are stressful. Think of it as a survival strategy (or flight response) to ensure they stay safe and that the impact on their well-being is minimised.

As you are aware, stress can be very difficult to manage for people with autism; they are in danger of shutdown, meltdown or even burnout. Every autistic person will do whatever they can to avoid these situations. Understand, autistic refusal is not the same as a three-year-old saying no, and you will never be able to bring the mountain to Mohammed. Rather, think of it as a lack of capacity rather than refusal, just like that flashing red LED when your car is about to run out of petrol. Most people in this state may want to engage, but just can't.

Here are some examples of how autistic people explain refusal to non-autistic people:

> *'Most of the situations are caused by non-autistic people never listening, making light of important things and refusing to make very simple and reasonable adjustments. Even when they make an unreasonable adjustment, they determine what it is in a take or leave it fashion and probably do it begrudgingly.'*

> *'For me, it happens when I'm nearing burnout. It was stuff like calling into work because I couldn't make myself get out of bed, or because I had gotten sick (which happened EVERY time I was pushed into a normal NT baseline of performance).'*

> *'Did this recently. It's "unable to", not "don't want to". And some of it is just the other person needing to adjust their thinking and automatic replies. Even if it's explained really well, if the other person refuses to accept it, it could still be seen as "just excuses".'*

> *'In a series of 'nots' I think. It's not a tantrum, it's not a control attempt, they're not trying to have a go at you.'*

Some people have a zero tolerance of refusal. For example, I always refuse to complete ethnicity and other monitoring sections of forms because of a conversation I had with a Holocaust survivor. It is something I can never be convinced to complete because it is simply wrong in my opinion. Many professional people get uppity because of my refusal, and some even see it as their right to know. Imagine how they'd react to your loved one's refusal if my simple 'none of your business' provokes such a strong reaction. Think about your loved one's refusals, and ask yourself whether the reaction it provokes is justified and, moreover, whether it's worth endangering their well-being?

Refusal can include certain foods, beverages, people, environments and opinions. So, what do you do when you have a refusal? There is no single answer and responding will always depend on context and your loved one's state at that moment.

On our journey, certain foods have been especially troublesome. Like many parents, we tried the 'no pudding if you don't eat your cauliflower, greens etc' approach. In every instance, it never worked, and we quickly adapted. Some food is better than none, in our opinion. With kindness and patience, Joe now eats a huge variety of food. The lesson here is to leave it for another day – making a battle of it only makes matters worse and those foods will forever be off the menu.

School refusal is a big issue for many parents and is the classic example of non-autistic people believing they know best. Many schools these days have zero-tolerance policies on uniform compliance, behaviour and conversation. Breaching any of the petty rules can result in sanctions, including being locked in a cell (sorry, 'exclusion room'). Repeat offending may result in suspension or permanent exclusion. When you approach a school about their treatment of your loved one, please be mindful of the law. The law trumps every policy and sanction they have, despite of what they may say.

Many autistic people have sensory issues and other issues surrounding clothing. Many uniform rules fail to accommodate these needs and are either penalising autistic people for non-compliance or forcing them to endure a sensory hell every day. Adjusting (not relaxing) the rules is not difficult and ensures the school is compliant with discrimination legislation. Joe's middle school had a uniform policy that required a certain brand of plain black socks. Joe never liked them, and always preferred colour. The head was unmoveable, but the SENCO wasn't and as she said, 'black socks are black socks, and if they have a motif on them no one will notice'. That simple compromise made a huge difference.

I know of children who have been dragged into school by staff. The tearful and distraught child has literally been torn from their parents' arms. The parents have tolerated this because they believed what they were told by the professionals. One particular child was ashamed of not being able to keep up with their peers and the jibes that came with it. The anxiety was simply dismissed as "low", and the parents were reassured that the child quickly settled in school. The parents acted when the child started self-harming. Imagine the message this sends to a vulnerable child. Also, what learning will a distressed child achieve?

Many autistic people need to stim to stay afloat and, as we have explored, some teaching staff class this as disruptive. However, continual masking to contain the need to stim and fit in with the school environment comes at a huge personal cost. Children have been sanctioned for quietly stimming because a teacher rather than students found it distracting. Sanctions for such disruption include isolation booths and suspension. I do wonder sometimes if some teachers and other staff know anything about autism and ADHD at all.

> To help Joe manage his stims, he kept a fidget toy in a trouser pocket. Every teacher in primary and senior school accepted this as a reasonable compromise and adjustment, except one primary head. This head was obnoxious, and I recall he chastised Joe more than once for having a hand in a pocket. That episode had a long-term effect on Joe, and it required six months of CAHMS before he recovered. Joe became withdrawn and, when we learnt about it, we saw the SENCO. I recall that the SENCO apologised and left us in her office for a short while she went next door to the head. All I can say is that I wouldn't like to get on the wrong side of that lady.

Every school has bullies and those headteachers that say they don't are deluded. Autistic people are easy targets for bullies, as I have described elsewhere. The expectation of being bullied can add an autistic child's stress. The constant drip, drip, drip will accumulate and eventually prove too much, and the autistic child will break. Everyone has a flight, fight or freeze response. Refusal is that flight mode on steroids. I was told a story a little while ago about an autistic girl who was beaten up daily. One day she snapped and took a knife into school to protect herself. Luckily, a teacher saw and confiscated the knife and obviously that young lady was suspended. I don't know if any sanctions were applied to the bully.[4]

While we have never had school refusal, I can share three stories that illustrate how complete refusal can be.

> Joe had swimming lessons for many years and enjoyed the activity. Originally, we had lessons to ensure his safety in the water, but it developed into something Joe thoroughly enjoyed until a temporary coach appeared. The new coach decided Joe needed to do racing turns and swim competitively. The coach refused to listen to my partner and tried forcing Joe. The coach didn't believe the warning about autism. The more the coach cajoled and bullied, the less Joe listened. Joe decided no more swimming, and no amount of support could change his mind.

---

4   Personal correspondence.

> Scouts were very supportive of Joe. Joe went through Beavers to Cubs and onto Scouts. In his Scout group there was a bully who turned up periodically leaving a trail of destruction in his wake. One day, he turned his attention to Joe and that was the last day Joe attended Scouts. No matter how it was presented, Scouts was a no-go area from that day.
>
> One Christmas, Joe worked as a Post Office temp. He was joined at the local depot by a neighbour. My neighbour lasted one day but Joe completed the contract and was offered a full-time role. Joe declined because of an opinionated manager who was forever chastising staff to work harder etc. Joe said six weeks was possible, but a lifetime was never possible because of the anxiety the manager created. Joe never wants to work in such an environment ever again.

Refusal is something autistic people encounter daily. Many organisations and services refuse access to autistic people. Mental health services regularly refuse to support autistic people and routinely use autism as the refusal excuse.

Refusal is something we should do on our loved one's behalf when councils and government departments put threshold hoops in the way. There are regulations to protect your loved ones, use them when appropriate.

A local authority demanded a 'blood sample' from my friend's profoundly autistic loved one for an SEN assessment. My friend asked why, and when no valid reason was given, he refused because of the trauma it would cause his loved one. The LA continued to demand and refused to assess his loved one until the blood sample was taken. This was despite the sharing of the relevant medical evidence with the LA. Eventually, the LA made an assessment without a blood sample.

On our journey, I have refused a face-to-face PIP assessment for Joe because of the consequences. I have used the PIP regulations to protect Joe.

Pain

As you have learnt by now, autistic people do things differently to non-autistic people, and how they feel pain is different to how everyone else experiences pain. One of the false stereotypes about autism is the inability to feel pain. Recent research confirms that the opposite is true, and in fact autistic people's pain perception is different to the non-autistic population and most feel pain at a higher intensity and are less adaptable to the sensation. This contrasts with their ability to withstand cold and heat etc. This creates a paradox that many fail to understand.

For example, when Joe is in pain it is the focus of everything. Its elimination is the only immediate task. Joe describes the pain as explosive and of an intensity that eliminates all other thoughts. From my own journey, this description sounds like a vomit-inducing migraine.

For some autistic people, estimating how much pain they are in is difficult. Many medics usually ask people to estimate how much pain they are in on a 1-10 scale. Because of sensory and other issues, the value given by an autistic person may underestimate the amount of pain they are in. Some may also not notice pain at all. Vale Giovanardi describes this phenomenon: 'It goes from "that leaf lightly brushing my arm feels like a sharp knife" to "I didn't notice I was resting my arm on a fryer until I smelled fried meat".'

Many autistic people struggle to quantify and qualitatively describe what they are enduring. Many autistic people describe acute pain as dysregulating. 'Safari' explains that she is, 'Very good at ignoring acute pain, dysregulated by chronic pain. I'm in pain daily mostly. Sometimes my pain is felt like my emotions.'

'CriticalFtw' explains that:

> 'Toothache is the worst, but I don't realise when I have cut myself, I've even had stitches once with no anaesthetic, if in pain I cannot concentrate on anything else other than the pain but explaining the level to someone is very difficult due issues communicating effectively.'

With the increasing prevalence of tele-health, clinicians who are unaware that autistic people feel pain differently may recommend an inappropriate course of treatment. For example, appendicitis is sometimes confused with indigestion, wind or constipation.

Fixations

Some autistic people can become fixated on certain things. These can become recurring themes and are sometimes triggers that drive behaviour. The fixation is usually linked to an experience that led to a loss of control. It is possible to mitigate to avoid the worst consequences. Some fixations are short lived while others are lifelong and may be trauma reactions.

> A few years ago, Joe suffered a nasty insect sting on his hand. From that point on, all insects were potential sources of further stings. We were able to mitigate this with a plug-in insect repellent and an explanation of antihistamines. Recently, when Joe was again bitten by an insect and his hand swelled as before, instead of losing control Joe went to a pharmacy and bought some antihistamine cream – a result of short-term mitigations and follow-up conversations.

Fixations need you to be adaptable and creative in your short-term mitigations. Each comes with a long-term solution; in this case, the plug-in was the mitigation and the discussion on antihistamines was the solution.

Unintended consequences

Autistic people are at a higher risk of experiencing traumatic events. You may wonder what that means; simply, that adverse events that a non-autistic person may find difficult but take in their stride may have long-term consequences for autistic people. Two recent studies (Griffiths et al, 2019; Rumball, 2019) concluded that autistic adults are more likely than the same age non-autistic people to develop PTSD or a mental health condition from adverse events.

While most difficult situations won't lead to the development of a mental health condition, they can develop a subconscious association with, for example, a sensory overload that adversely affects behaviour later. Adverse events can include responses to sensory overload, confrontation and isolation.

> About a decade ago, Joe was stopped from leaving an exam by an invigilator. Joe overheats when it is warm, and this causes considerable distress that can lead to meltdown or shutdown. Obviously, the invigilator

was enforcing exam regulations while totally ignorant of Joe's needs. To mitigate distress in school, we purchased two silent fans for the school 'base' and a portable A/C unit for Joe's bedroom. However, we were unaware of the depth of the consequences. Over the years, this fixation with warm weather has festered, and every warm night would mean no sleep for anyone. The mitigation for this was permanently installed A/C. The consequence of that invigilator's 'no' is still with us. We only understood the depth of this fixation recently.

Rebecca describes the impact a teacher had on her:

> *'My teacher shouted at me in year one for talking, it absolutely terrified me and was enough to completely stop me speaking in class for five years. That's one of a countless number of adverse events that had lasting negative impacts.'*

Invisibility and disability

Autism is invisible. This simple statement encompasses so much of autism; what it is to be autistic, the consequences and life chances. Autistic invisibility touches on notions of disability, behaviour, personal preference and access to support.

While society has become more aware of autism, it is still indifferent and or ignorant of autistic people and those who support them, and many autistic people feel excluded. This invisibility is reflected in the statistics; for example, the official prevalence figure has been 1/100 for 20 years despite three DSM updates in that time. A recent paper published in *The Lancet* estimated the prevalence was 1/34 (O'Nions *et al*, 2023).

Being invisible is sometimes how many autistic people prefer to be. Given their journeys, many feel it is easier and safer. Joe once said he'd like a Harry Potter invisibility cloak so he can hide when he's had enough of others.

In recent years, however, things have started to change for the better, due to the campaigning and advocacy of others. Many businesses have realised the innovation that autistic people can create, and many colleges and universities offer appropriate support more readily.

Is autism a disability?

Autism is complex, and because of that it can be profoundly disabling for people with complex and high-dependency needs, while on the other hand, for a small minority it may only occasionally be disabling. Obviously, with severe or profound autism there are visible and auditory indications of something different, but for many people, there is no visible indication of disability. Because autism is invisible to most people, many do not see it as a disability and this consequently makes autism more disabling. There is the German concept of 'Leidendruck' (pressure of suffering) that explains this phenomenon.

Many people, including some local authority officers, assume that because there is no visible sign of a disability, like a wheelchair, a person is faking. This is also complicated by masking, where a person hides their autism. That said, a SENCo I respect once said, 'If you take your time and observe, there are always subtle visible signs'. Moreover, if my granddaughter can spot autism in her nursery, why is it so hard for others?

Autism can be made disabling by context and environment. This is especially true for autistic people who are hyper-sensitive (over- sensitive) rather than hypo-sensitive (under- sensitive). For example, Joe is sensitive to busy and noisy places. To manage this, we always board an aircraft first, so it fills up around us.

Some autistic people say Asperger's Syndrome is the only acceptable form of autism in society. If you think about it, you may understand why some autistic people say autism itself isn't disabling, but that it's society that makes it profoundly disabling.

Autism is a protected trait under the UK's Equality Act 2010 and is classed as a disability by the government. There is a specific Autism Act, with devolved nations having additional legislation and frequently updated strategies. The legislation creates statutory duties on organisations, and statutory guidance clearly states what is expected.

On this journey, disability laws have proved helpful in overcoming local authority and DWP hurdles. Framing important questions, and especially when challenging gatekeeping decisions (denying access to services) as disability discrimination does help when backed up by quotes from the statutory guidance or appropriate Acts.

Some autistic people say that autism is a disability that has seriously affected their lives. Joe has occasionally described autism as 'a massive pain in the arse'. An anonymous autistic person explained that they see it 'as a disability because it has seriously impacted on my quality of life'.

Jess Plant simply says, 'For me, it is a disability'.

Some autistic people look at disability quite differently from most people, seeing it as something that is done to them by society and people who are ignorant. This is best illustrated by their own words. 'Lambent Monkey' explains:

> *'I want to say "no" because neurodivergence is a difference, not brokenness. However, given the society we live in, Autism is incredibly disabling. So in our current experience, yes, I feel it is effectively a disability'.*

Simon explained, 'Not a broken computer, but a different operating system'.

Carla Stacey describes how an environment affects her:

> *'I am disabled by my environment, I do not "have a disability".'*

Other autistic people see autism as their superpower as it enables them to develop niche skills, with it being described as 'an ability' that provides 'a different slant on common perception', or that is has 'some advantages, like my memory and hyperlexia'.

The majority accept that autism is a double-edged sword and generally dynamic in nature. Edward Phillips's response is typical of many:

> *'Yes [it is a disability] (and in the UK legally) though for me a very dynamic one... Some days I feel on top of the world other days barely able to drag myself out of bed...'*

Carla Painter goes further and explains why support is important:

> *'Maybe if you have the right support, it's no longer disabling, but most people don't need those supports to function.'*

Social interaction

Social interaction is complex and includes non-verbal communication, the subtle but indecipherable hints non-autistic people make with their tone of voice and body language. Like a significant number of non-autistic people, autistic people often have difficulty 'reading' or interpreting others. This can include difficulty in recognising or understanding others' feelings and intentions and expressing their own emotions.

This can make it very hard to navigate the non-autistic social world. It basically comes down to those meaningless etiquette rules that non-autistic people seem to value. As a consequence, many autistic people may:

- appear to be insensitive
- seek out time alone when overloaded by other people
- not seek comfort from other people
- appear to behave in a socially unacceptable way
- find it hard to form friendships

To give some balance to this deficit, I asked my autistic followers on Twitter 'what has autism taught you about non-autistic people?'. I had two themes in the replies, one that shows how far we have still to go and one that shows how far we have already come. Some replies were extensive and explained everything in detail; for brevity, I have included shortened versions:

> *'They will look down on me for not being like them.'*

> *'As an autistic minority, it is not unreasonable to feel like you understand others than they understand life as an autistic.'*

> *'[Non-autistic people] only comprehend others based on their own experience and struggle to empathise with alternative thought processing.'*

Some replies were direct, as you'd expect, and included, 'They lie', 'Social norms aren't normal', and 'I prefer animals'.

The replies showing progress came mainly from parents saying how proud they were of their loved ones and how much they had changed for the better.

Loneliness

Loneliness is complex and is a response to social and emotional isolation. A person can be lonely even when they are surrounded by others. The CDC has recently said that loneliness can shorten lives (National Academies of Science, 2020), and loneliness is also linked to depression and other mental health issues (Barber, 2018).

An autistic licensed counsellor, Jessica Penot, 2023, explains: 'In listening, I have observed many variables that seem to cause the most chronic despair in people with autism. One of the most universal variables is *loneliness*. Every adult or adolescent client I work with that has autism struggles with profound loneliness and a sense of isolation.'

Most autistic people will have endured or are enduring periods of extreme loneliness. The consequences are complex, but the causes are relatively simple, the assumptions of others. Autistic people try to fit into a world designed for others, despite their unique way of being in the world.

Some describe their experiences of being ostracised, blanked or classed as 'too serious to have fun' or simply 'hard work'. One thing I have noticed is how many people simply don't bother to contact their autistic 'friends' – it always appears to me that the autistic person must always make the first move. Think how that may make someone feel and ask whether it emphasises the belief that they are of no consequence to others. This is probably caused by a lack of awareness and those invisible but elastic rules that non-autistic folk love.

Even autistic people are guilty of this, having seen it myself, where newcomers try to become involved in social groups meant for autistic people. Over the years, an autistic person can only take so much rejection, so much being left out. Loneliness becomes the norm, the default holding pattern.

Some autistic people decide it is easier to be lonely than to struggle with others. The cost to themselves destroys what is left of them. As a carer, I occasionally choose solitude to preserve what is left of my soul, so I get this aspect of autism. There is plenty of evidence to support this phenomenon with autistic people.

Acceptance/Awareness days

Each year the UN tries to increase awareness and acceptance of autism through its 'World Autism Awareness Day'. Little by little, the campaigns chip away at ignorance and indifference, and slowly things improve.

You may ask why is this important, so ask yourself how prejudice is overcome. I'll let Marie Martin give the answer: 'If I see I have a flat tyre, I am aware of it. If I think about it and realise that I cannot drive with a flat tyre, I understand it. If I change my tyre, or get the RAC to come and help, I accept it.'

Many charities and activists coordinate their campaigns around this time to raise money to enable them to continue their work, supporting autistic people, lobbying for legislative changes and increasing awareness.

Many autistic people dislike the yearly 'awareness train' because all the deficits are highlighted and 'how hard my life is' celebrities that appear in the media, and the benefits are rarely the focus. Moreover, the 'with autism' and 'autistic' vaccine epidemic conspiracy and cure arguments come to the fore and can reinforce other people's prejudice. However, without the coordinated media attention, how much progress would have been made in increasing acceptance? How many legislative changes would there have been? So, every April, remember to mention autism to strangers, your work colleagues, your family. Remember to respectfully 'stick it to your elected representatives'. Remind everyone of the considerable contribution autistic people have made to human progress.

Over the years, these campaigns have improved access to services for autistic people by creating social pressure. You may recall the National Autistic Society's (NAS) campaign for shops to have quiet hours when autistic and other folk with sensory needs could go shopping. The idea was simple: shops would turn down their lights, music and announcements for an hour. Obviously, this benefits very many people. Almost all large supermarkets now do a quieter hour. Some would say, however, they are tokenistic because they are uncoordinated and at inconvenient times.

More recently, the NAS and other charities have used Awareness Days to lobby for reform of the UK Mental Health Act (1983), which significantly disadvantages autistic people. The coordinated effort has resulted in significant improvements in the proposed replacement legislation.

Remember, though, that every day is an 'awareness day' for an autistic person, so always spread a little acceptance and awareness wherever you are every day.

Prevalence

Prevalence is the measure of autistic people in the general population. The actual number varies by area, ethnicity, class, country and gender. Prevalence is important because using an old figure ensures that support is either non-existent or too insignificant, leading to inadequate and oversubscribed services.

Prevalence changes with time, and understanding that change can ensure policy and budgets change to reflect future needs. Obviously, an increasing prevalence of autism is controversial, but this should not detract from ensuring people's needs are met. We need to remember that autism prevalence is a lagging measure, that is it is always out of date.

The fact is that prevalence is complicated. Different organisations will use different ways to arrive at a figure, and these figures certainly underestimate the true number of autistic people because they generally only include those with a formal diagnosis. The figures will exclude those who are self-diagnosed, those waiting for a diagnosis and, obviously, those who don't know they are autistic.

For quite a long time, autism prevalence has 'officially' stood at 1%, or one in a hundred people. In the UK, there is apparently no official figure but this figure is usually cited. In the past, I have asked ministers, via my MP, about prevalence and was told it is something that is looked after by the National Autistic Society (NAS). However, the NAS, while maintaining a 1% figure on its website, say it's a government matter. So, as usual, everyone simply says it's someone else's responsibility.

Anecdotally, the rate in the UK appears to be about 1/30 (most classes have about one autistic child). In early 2023, the 'Center for Disease Control' or CDC in the USA reported a prevalence of 1/36 among eight-year-olds. A recent report in *The Lancet* suggests the rate was 1/34 in England. O'Nions *et al* (2023) also suggest a UK prevalence of 1/34. These agree with anecdotal findings. Interestingly, the government in Northern Ireland reported that prevalence was 5%, or 1/20 (Department of Health, 2023). The report stated that 7.3% of boys and 2.7% of girls were autistic.

The baseline prevalence figure hides the complexity of the spectrum. The Centre for Disease Control in the US suggests that:

- 40% of autistic people are non-verbal.
- 31% have a learning disability.
- 44% have above-average intelligence.

The baseline figure also ignores the disparities found in the prevalence when broken down into male and female statistics, culture and ethnicity. Currently, boys are three to four times more likely to be diagnosed as autistic than girls.

A few years ago, I had a meeting with the head of service (and others) at my local authority. One of my memories from that meeting is the lack of disclosure of the prevalence used to size services. I was left with the impression that prevalence varies and depends on context, and there was no breakdown of the figures by context. This makes me worry, because it suggests that autism is an elastic diagnosis that contracts or expands to fit a budget or bid.

Many years ago, my previous MP, Dr Starkey, bravely attended a meeting of the local Autism Parents Group to listen to our issues. As an outcome of the meeting, she asked my LA how many autistic people they knew of. She was shocked by their response of two, given that there were at least 30 parents present at the meeting, and that meeting was held in a school for autistic children.

Many people will use an increasing prevalence to say there are too many autistic people being diagnosed. For example, many people point to the Amish community in the United States and claim that there no instances of autism. It is an interesting point, but those claiming this forget how Amish life is constructed and how Amish people interact with the outside world – Amish life has considerable levels of structure and predictability. Robinson et al (2010) have indicated that autism is in fact present in the community.

Recent increases in prevalence have led to many overlapping and sometimes contradictory theories. Some people claim that the yearly increase in prevalence points to an epidemic of autism. Many forget that the definition of autism has evolved and the number of clinicians aware of and diagnosing autism has increased, while there has been a steady decline in the number of diagnoses of other conditions.

Russel (2021) concluded that the 'Increases could be due to growth in prevalence or, more likely, increased reporting and application of diagnosis. Rising diagnosis among adults, females and higher functioning individuals suggest augmented recognition underpins these changes.'

It is also possible to see the change in prevalence as socially based rather than biological with an environmental cause (Gerrard, 2022). Consider how society has evolved through the lenses of politics and sociology, causing a rise in autism at the expense of other diagnosed conditions. It could be argued that autism is more socially acceptable than previous diagnoses.

Culture, societal and community perceptions can also have a large impact on prevalence rates. For example, some assume only boys get autism and that is reflected in the 4:1 ratio of boys to girls. Kim (2012) and Pham *et al* (2022) discuss this complex issue in greater detail.

Origins and myths

The discovery of autism and the myths surrounding it have cast a long shadow. That shadow has had profound consequences for the acceptance of autistic people and those who support them. That shadow includes parental blame and assumptions about the personalities of people with autism and their abilities. The shadow also hides the contribution many autistic people have made to human progress.

Some people believe the traits that combine to form autism are new, but others argue that autism is part of the human condition. Indeed, researchers such as O'Connel & Fitzgerald (2014) have considered historical figures such as Alan Turing and suggested that they may have been autistic. Dr Temple Gradin once said: 'What would happen if the autism gene was eliminated from the gene pool? You would have a bunch of people standing around in a cave, chatting and socializing and not getting anything done.'

A short history of autism

The term 'autistic' was first used in 1908 to describe schizophrenic people who were very withdrawn. In 1924, a Russian psychologist Grunya Sukhareva characterised autism nearly two decades before it was 'discovered' by Leo Kanner and Hans Asperger. In 1925, Sukhareva published a paper describing the lives of the children she supported. Her explanations are like those in DSM 5 and ICD 11. Sukhareva's work first appeared in English in 2013.

In the early 1920s, psychiatrist Georg Frankl and psychologist Anni Weiss started working at Heilpädagogik Children's Clinic in Vienna. Both published papers in the 1930s that described children in ways that we would know today as autistic. Hans Asperger joined the clinic in the early 1930s and trained under Weiss and Frankl. Frankl and Weiss, both Jewish, emigrated to the US as the situation in Austria deteriorated under the Nazis. Frankl was hired by Leo Kanner and became a key part of Kanner's children's clinic. Leo Kanner became a pioneer of early autism research.

While it is difficult to speculate on the roles of Frankl and Weiss in helping Kanner and Asperger formulate their ideas, it is more than a coincidence that both pioneers benefitted from their knowledge.

Asperger coined the term 'little professors' to describe the children he wrote about. Many forget that Asperger worked in the clinic in Vienna where some of the founders of Aktion T4 (the Nazi euthanasia programme) worked. A recent paper (Czech, 2018) has in fact alleged (in the legal sense) that he sent children to T4.

After World War 2, Suhkareva, Kanner and Asperger recognised that autism was a separate condition to schizophrenia, however Suhkareva was the only one to understand that the condition was rooted in different brain development. All three read and published in the same journals but it is difficult to say whether Kanner and Asperger benefitted from Suhkareva's work.

Kanner wrote his 'landmark' paper on autism in 1943. Kanner was probably the origin of most of the mother-blaming theories that still exist to this day (Crowell *et al*, 2019). Kanner suggested that there was little warmth in the parents of autistic children. This and the work of others lead to Bettelheim's 'Theory of Autism'. Bettelheim (1967) went further and compared autism to being a prisoner in a concentration camp. The colloquial term 'refrigerator mothers' originates from this time (Waltz, 2015).

In the 1970s, Lorna Wind and Judith Gould believed that there were more autistic people present in society than those predicted by Kanner. Their research concluded that autism is a spectrum of traits rather than the single condition described by Kanner, and it was the combination of these traits that defined an individual's autism.

Some of the stereotypes, myths and confusions surrounding autism originate with these pioneers. Imagine where we would have been if Suhkareva's ideas were adopted instead of Kanner's and Asperger's.

Culture

Culture is usually defined as all the ways of life, including the arts, beliefs and institutions of a population that are passed down from generation to generation. Culture includes codes of manners, dress, language, religion, rituals, art, myths, politics, acceptance of authority, tolerance, assumptions, stereotypes etc.

Some cultural influences originate in deliberate policies to enforce conformity and can remain strong despite being proven wrong. Many years ago, for example, there was a deliberate policy to enforce right-handedness, and made assumptions that were made about people who were left-handed had a huge negative impact.

You may wonder what culture has to do with autism, but in fact culture has an instrumental impact on autism. Subtle differences in culture can entirely change outcomes for autistic people. Consider how those invisible social rules are used to demonstrate that autistic people have social communication deficits, but the truth is far more complicated and involves instant judgements by non-autistic people, tribal behaviour, fear of anything different etc.

Think of the assumptions you make when you meet someone new. You might look at the quality of their clothes, how their hair is done, how they speak, the car they drive etc. But the clothes could be borrowed, their sister could be a hairdresser, and they could be up to their eyeballs in debt to pay for the flash car. I once read a story about Warren Buffet, a very successful businessman, who wanted to buy a new car for a loved one. Mr Buffet drove to a garage, but the salesman took one look at Mr Buffet's tired but trusty old pickup truck and assumed he could not afford a new car…

Some cultures value community while others value individuals. This fundamental difference can have profound consequences for autistic people and their families. Individualistic cultures may recognise autism more readily and have some autism-related services. Community-based cultures, on the other hand, may stigmatise difference more but may have services to support families. Cultures can vary widely even within the same country.

Basic and common traits or early indicators of autism may not raise concern in some cultures. Eye contact is important in Western cultures, but in some Asian cultures direct eye contact with those in authority is avoided because it is considered disrespectful. In India, it is assumed that boys generally start talking later than girls and parents don't worry until a child is four. Moreover, in some Western cultures, a three-year-old girl who doesn't mix well with children of her own age but engages well with adults may be considered mature. Similarly, a quiet child who plays quite happily on their own may be described as a 'good' child.

Socio and economic factors are also significant in that wealthier people will have the time and means to access services. Some cultures have considerable stigma associated with mental illness. For example, in Chinese culture, many parents feel ashamed of having a disabled child with some believing that it is a punishment for the parents' behaviour, especially the mother's. Moreover, social pressure in Chinese culture expects conformity and appears to have little tolerance for an individual's differences. A discussion of these issues from a clinical perspective can be found in Bernier (2010).

Historically, there has been a cultural assumption that autism is more prevalent in boys than girls. This is reflected in the ratio of diagnoses between the sexes. Outdated stereotypes around how boys and girls are supposed to act feed into this perception and create a cultural expectation that girls are somehow more immune to autism. Wigdor *et al* (2022) discuss the 'female protective effect' in detail.

Culturally, autism is seen through a lens of deficits because of the medicalised approach to diagnosis which describes it as a disorder with historical false links to schizophrenia, and which frames it in legalisation as a mental illness (UK Mental Health Act 1983 is an example). These obscure the positive characteristics of autism that contribute to human diversity and creativity, enable profound progress in the arts and sciences, and social progress to a more inclusive society. The traits that combine to form autism only become a disorder when society defines them as such, and a resultant disability when the social environment cannot accommodate them.

When autism was first postulated in the early 20th century by medical professionals, think about how their discoveries were framed; Kanner's Syndrome and Asperger's Syndrome etc. Take a moment to consider whether that says more about these pioneers than the traits they 'discovered'. Think about how these pioneers initially described autism as a type of schizophrenia and the long cultural shadow that has been cast as a result.

In the early 20th century, people perceived to be mentally ill people were usually institutionalised. These people were usually described as a burden on society. This practice has cultural implications in how we deal with mental health and neurodivergence today. Our daily language is full of references about how 'crazy' people are treated, such as being 'carted off to the funny farm by men in white coats'... The practice has even influenced the emojis people use 🤪. The use of institutions still impacts how society treats those who need a little TLC, and this is evident in the burden-laden language used by many politicians and the media.

A story that illustrates this point is the early life of Dr Temple Grandin. Dr Grandin writes that her parents were advised to place her in an institution and forget about her. Dr Grandin's parents disagreed and patiently helped their daughter become the world-famous animal husbandry expert she has become (and an icon in the autism community) (Britannia, 2024).

I could continue to write endlessly about how the medicalisation of autism and how its framing has cast a long and very dark shadow over autism. That shadow seriously impacts the life chances of our loved ones and has caused needless pain, suffering and death.

Genetics and heritability

One of the recurring disagreements when it comes to autism is its cause. There are many different opinions and some are controversial, and sometimes these contribute to the 'shadow'.

The genetic basis of autism is strong but complex and, despite a huge effort, it remains unclear whether autism is explained by multi-gene interactions or by rare mutations with major effects.

Heritability is a measure of how differences in genes account for differences in traits, like eye colour and whether they are left or right-handed, for example. Traits can also be things that make some people autistic. Heritability is basically a comparison of genetic influence and environmental influence in determining the variability of a trait across a population. A value of one indicates that the cause is genetic and a value of zero indicates that the cause is environmental.

Studies of twins have suggested that autism has a heritability score of 90% (Sandin *et al*, 2017). Personally, I believe in genetics, but please do your own research.

Myths

Autism has many myths associated with it. Many are associated with the perceived causes of autism, some are based on the assumptions people make based on stereotypes, and others are based on unproven or disproven theories.

Vaccines Paracetamol Rude & Cold **Autism Myths** No empathy Mercury Glysophate **RIGID**

Several years ago, *Forbes* magazine published an article about things some people associate with autism (Willingham, 2013). One of the more interesting of these was the suggestion that autism was caused by 'too much money'. The article also touched on the greatest myth of all: vaccines.

Many years ago, a doctor claimed that the MMR vaccine causes autism. The doctor was later discredited. Newspapers and other media hyped the story and pushed it until it became self-perpetuating. Fitzpatrick (2005), writing in *The BMJ*, discusses this issue in detail. Many scientists have debunked the myth time and time again. Recently, a study in Denmark with over 500,000 children concluded that there is no link between the MMR vaccine and autism (Tanne, 2022).

I have deliberately only focused on the vaccine myth to illustrate how a myth may be deconstructed. Always be a little sceptical and do your own independent research using reputable sources.

Chapter 3:
Practical advice

This chapter is all about you and how you apply your mindset, purpose, and resilience to reduce the influence of those who make your journey difficult. This is where you will discover your inner Viking.

As you already know, autism doesn't make your journey difficult – it is other people and organisations and the policies and systems they employ that make life hard. This may seem daunting, like driving in a foreign country without a satnav, but I guarantee you will find many diversions and shortcuts left by other carers.

These carer shortcuts will hopefully be instructive in:

- How you deal with bureaucracy.
- How you support your loved one.
- How you access services.
- How you plan for the best and prepare for the worst.
- How you plan for the future.

Diagnosis

For many, this is a complex and emotional decision. There is doubt and worry about the process and the impact of clinical outcomes. This is normal.

Many are worried about the stigma of a 'label', which can feel like a millstone around your neck. You may feel that your loved one would make greater progress if they were not restricted by a label. Many are also worried about the impact a label may have on their lives and how others will perceive you and yours.

Those worried about diagnostic labels should be aware of the labels other people may also attach to their loved one. Some people, including their peers, may perceive your loved one as naughty, etc. Some of these labels may be sticky.

Some people will tell you that extra help in schools is not dependent on a diagnosis. While that may be true in an ideal world, it is very dependent on you, a motivated teacher, a motivated school, and a helpful LA. Support is supposed to be provided for a child's individual needs, however the needs of an autistic child are quite different to those of a child with ADHD, for example. How is a teacher supposed to provide the correct support without knowing the clinical needs of your child?

If you have no experience of autism, a diagnosis can help you understand your loved one's needs and how you can support them. A diagnosis can assist in bypassing some of the hoops that the system will put in your way, and help you get past the gatekeepers that may appear on your journey. Some people describe a diagnosis as a roadmap (to ensure the best possible outcomes) (Palumbo, 2022).

Early diagnosis, in my opinion, enables earlier support and intervention. It will hopefully ensure a decent education and avoid many of the 'lost years' that many late-diagnosed adults describe. Early diagnosis also reduces the risk of mental health and social difficulties (Mandy *et al*, 2022).

When you first notice

The birth of a loved one is a joyous moment, and gives you a feeling that can't really be described. Joe is our youngest and the experience of coping with a child was not new to us. That said, there were little differences that, with hindsight and knowledge, are clear indicators of a difference. For example, Joe didn't like cuddles, he preferred to feed himself, eye contact was different, he wouldn't eat any baby food, and routine was *king*.

Many people advise that a routine is important with any baby and Joe was no different, but with Joe it was more so. For example, there was a five-minute window to put Joe down to sleep, and if the window was missed, we endured four hours of an upset baby. As Joe became a toddler, it was clear he was quite different to his siblings. At some point we thought Joe was spoilt; spoilt with attention and spoilt materially. We listened to the health visitor's reassurances.

Many people first really learn their loved one is different when they start nursery or school. Joe was no different. He was rarely any trouble, but once in nursery he pushed a teacher who had got too close. We were summoned and Joe apologised. He was full of remorse. The staff knew why Joe was different, but they wouldn't tell us. Eventually, a 'brave' teacher took us aside and suggested we go to a local Speech & Language Therapy (SLT) drop-in session. Joe's mum did as she asked and we eventually saw a paediatrician. At no point did anyone mention autism. Many other carers have similar stories of teachers voicing their concerns but never saying what they suspected. Knowing would have helped those of us who had never heard of autism.

If you realise your loved one is different but can't quite put your finger on it, talk quietly to other parents, but please don't compare your loved one to theirs. Remember, you can join a few local Facebook and other social media groups and just listen and learn.

When you first speak to a health professional about your loved one, they will initially try to reassure you. You may hear phrases like 'boys are slower', 'girls don't get autism' etc, but if you are not reassured you need to be persistent. A good starting point is a speech and language therapist.

Other parents and siblings of autistic people are very good at spotting autistic chidlren. They instinctively know. So, if you are unsure, ask those with lived experience in your family network or friendship circles.

I recall a trip to Spain for a holiday where a lad on the flight asked a few questions. Instantly we knew the young man was autistic. A polite and flight-long conversation with the lad's extended family confirmed our observation. They had made a similar observation of Joe.

Telling your loved one

Throughout this guide, I talk about singular people, some of whom were probably autistic. Many may not understand why, but it is part of my desire to change the narrative from disorder, burden and deficit to one of recognition and acceptance. This is important for many little people to know they are not alone and can contribute to progress and society.

A few years ago, I spoke to a mum and her autistic daughter who were really struggling because of how other people perceived the daughter and her profound interest in nature and books. I asked the young lady if she knew about Nobel Prizes and if she knew of the only person to win two. When she indicated that she didn't, I talked about Marie Curie. I gently explained that Curie was noted for being awkward, determined and having bad days. As she listened, an ever-increasing smile appeared.

My wife has a similar story about a football-mad autistic young man. My wife explained about Lionel Messi, a very famous and possibly autistic footballer.

Many parents may decide to hide any diagnosis from their loved ones to ensure they are not labelled. A distant friend of the family chose not to tell her autistic loved one until he was an adult, but when he went to university with no support, they nearly lost him.

From the outset, we have tried to be open with Joe about autism. We choose to avoid the deficits and focus on the positives, without accepting autism as an excuse. We discussed the 'how and when' for months and, when we asked our excellent CAHMS psychologist how to do it, her reply was simply: 'Now, he is clever and knows he is different, he wants answers. I can help with the answers.'

Supporting and caring for an autistic person depends ultimately on trust. Joe's psychologist believed that mutual trust is fundamental to ensure the best outcomes. Ask yourself whether you would trust someone who had hidden something fundamental from you.

Telling Joe was straightforward – we had lots of quiet conversations and added more detail at age-appropriate times. We did it this way because Joe is reserved and dislikes 'a fuss'. Also, Joe needs time to process.

When you decide to inform your loved one, do it when their life is relatively calm and stable so you can adjust to their changing mood. For example, avoid informing them at Christmas because of the likely overload and forever forming an association with that time of year.

The process

Autism is a bundle of traits, and a diagnosis looks for the presence of and the relationship between these traits. Many people assume that the diagnostic process is a tick-box exercise, but it is far more complicated. Whether the diagnosis is carried out by a supervising paediatrician, an extremely well and appropriately qualified nurse (MSc level) or a clinical psychologist, the process will be similar. A multi-discipline team of clinicians will contribute to the diagnosis.

Autism is defined in a clinical manual like DSM V or ICD 10/11. The manuals will describe and list the diagnostic traits and the thresholds associated with each trait.

Autism is diagnosed using tests derived from these manuals. Two prominent tests favoured by clinicians are the Autism Diagnostic Observation Schedule (ADOS) and the Autism Diagnostic Interview-Revised (ADI-R). These are behaviour focused. They are very reliable but are not as effective with women and ethnic minorities as they are with white men. The tests are indicative, but at the end of the day, an experienced clinician will be far more effective. The Diagnostic Interview of Social Communication (DISCO) test is also used in the UK.

The diagnosis process is complicated and may take years to complete from first referral. The diagnostic process consists of assessments, conversations and observations. Different medical and other professionals will talk to you and your loved one. Some may discretely observe your loved one play and their interactions with others. Each will report to a supervising clinician and contribute to a cumulative process that will arrive at a final diagnosis. Sometimes, a blood sample may be taken to rule out conditions like 'Fragile X'.

Sometimes, a clinician may ask for additional assessments to fine-tune their diagnosis. The initial diagnosis may not be as complete as it may miss significant comorbidities, like ADHD or OCD.

It is also possible to have a different diagnosis to the one you might expect, and you may wonder how this is possible. This can be as simple as the diagnostic pathway chosen, or the dynamic nature of autism and other conditions. The interaction between conditions can be very dynamic and one could be more prominent than another during an assessment. This dynamic nature can complicate matters significantly. For example, a friend's loved one was diagnosed with Asperger Syndrome as a child and was only diagnosed with comorbid ADHD as a young adult. You may recall the conflict between autism and ADHD described earlier.

Another friend's loved one was not diagnosed until age 16, despite being non-verbal with other profound needs. Over the years, many teachers and support workers had suggested this child had 'autistic tendencies', but no paediatrician would confirm a diagnosis. During childhood, Ritalin had been prescribed by a paediatrician, which suggests that ADHD was suspected. However, Ritalin turned the child into a catatonic zombie. When the child turned 16, the family finally got a diagnosis confirming the autism that was suspected all along. The clinician who confirmed the diagnosis was aghast that it had to take so long to diagnose what was 'blindingly obvious'.

Misdiagnosis or a missed diagnosis is also possible because of the dynamic nature of comorbidities and the inherent bias in some diagnostic tools and a clinician's own bias. For example, females are better at internalising symptoms which can lead to confusion with anxiety and depression. Gesi *et al* (2021) discuss this in detail.

Misdiagnosis or missed diagnosis is relatively common. A recent paper in *The Lancet* suggested that around a quarter of diagnoses may be perceived as incorrect (Kentrou *et al*, 2024). This rises to one-third for women. The most common misdiagnosis was 'personality disorder'. If you feel a clinician has got it wrong, ask them to explain the diagnosis in detail and how they came to their conclusion. If you are still unsure, ask the clinician to pause and re-evaluate their decision. On our journey, the diagnosing paediatrician initially thought classic autism, but after a pause and a re-evaluation following a long conversation with Joe about hydraulics, he revised his conclusion to Asperger Syndrome.

The aftermath

A diagnosis is just the beginning, but the aftermath of a diagnosis can be a very lonely place. When Joe was diagnosed, we were simply given a letter and a bundle of paper. We had no idea what to do, where to go, or who to talk to.

Some local authorities run parenting courses for parents of newly diagnosed children. These courses may only cover the very basics but may provide some very valuable initial signposting. Usually, these courses are run by Child Services or Sendias. It is worth reaching out to Sendias as they may be able to connect you with various parent groups. The local authority may also have an extensive 'local offering' of services on their website.

There are many Facebook parents and carers groups. Many of these are closed groups for obvious reasons, but most are worth joining and they will provide very effective signposting and camaraderie.

I would suggest that all newly diagnosed adults have some post-diagnosis therapy with an appropriate therapist to work through the considerable feelings that may surface. Some may have considerable anger, resentment or existential questions. I would caution against telling the outside world until your loved one is settled. Remember, many people, including employers and work colleagues, may not be as supportive as they should be.

Private or NHS

This is not as straightforward as it may at first seem, and it ultimately depends on the quality and completeness of the service offered. The single most important question is whether the diagnosis will be accepted by local authorities, government departments and the NHS.

The law says there is no difference between a private or an NHS diagnosis provided the report was written by specialist-trained, experienced and registered clinicians following an assessment process that includes a 'Gold standard' (like Autism Diagnostic Observation Schedule (ADOS-2) or Autism Diagnostic Interview (ADI-R)) that exceeds NICE guidelines.

To illustrate the point, the SEND (2015) code of practice is clear that there is no basis in law for an LA to reject a diagnostic report because it was privately obtained.

Obviously, with some families waiting up to four years for a diagnosis, the private option appears to be the only route. However, before deciding to go private, thoroughly evaluate your options.

Ask yourself whether:

- your loved one is thriving rather than just coping
- their school is meeting all your loved one's needs
- a speedier diagnosis will improve outcomes
- the practice is well established, with experienced and appropriately qualified and trained staff operating above NICE guidelines
- you can afford the cost of the diagnosis
- the clinic/clinician has an NHS or an LA diagnostic contract

The price of private assessments varies considerably. Locally, a private practice offers one from £800, but a family we know paid around £3,000. We had an NHS diagnosis, and it took two years to complete.

Social media has many stories in which an LA or school has refused to accept a diagnosis. There appears to be an assumption that a private clinician will give you what you 'need' because you are paying for it. Claire Churchill explains: 'I was told by the school that they couldn't act on a report from a very well-qualified clinician because I had paid for the assessments, and therefore they would have "just given me what I paid for".'

A clinician can lose their registration or licence to practice if they do this. It is also worth remembering that many 'private' clinicians also work for our NHS.

NHS guidance (from Direct.Gov) states, 'You're still entitled to free NHS care if you choose to pay for additional private care'. So, if it is good enough for our NHS and HM Government, it is good enough for your LA.

Angela Whitehead explains that she:

> 'had this issue years ago with dyslexia. Blown out of the water when I found the authority also used the same clinician for their work. It's just so rubbish.'

'Activist Lawyer' adds:

> '...16 years ago we arrived in the UK with my son's NZ Min of Health/Min of Ed ASD referral backed up by a NZ private paediatrician diagnosis (usual system). Not accepted by my LA. Fortunately, our UK GP quickly referred us through the NHS for a diagnosis...'

If you encounter any refusal, instantly push back and challenge it. Ask for the clinical reasons for the refusal. No other reasons are acceptable. Please remember, not all LAs behave in this fashion.

Listening (and reading)

Listening is a skill, many say, and it is a shame that many professionals never learn how to do it. As we have learnt, autism is complex and every autistic person is unique. Many can't communicate their wishes effectively because they may be non-verbal, situationally mute or just not in a good place at that moment.

Who is there to speak for them, to safeguard their safety, uphold their rights and their liberty and freedom? Generally, only family and friends will stand up for their own. Only family and friends will understand how their loved one ticks and what each nuance means. If a professional doesn't listen, the consequences may not be pleasant.

A friend's loved one suffers from IBS and my friend constantly reminds daycare support staff of the foods that will trigger an IBS outburst. One such food is cheese. Occasionally, the staff let my friend's loved one eat cheese and it's guaranteed that a few hours later they phone for clean clothes.

Many of the issues that arise are because professionals never read the notes or make notes when they are listening. Their notes usually list a few things that are triggering and state why you should never do something in a certain way. It always appears that it is your fault for them messing up, but it is because they are simply too lazy to read first.

I know of a profoundly autistic gentleman with learning disabilities who is triggered by strangers in the family home, and the consequences the family suffer including little sleep until he resettles. The gentleman's parents have ensured that everyone knows of these restrictions and always request that people who need to visit always do it when their loved one is at his day centre or in respite. Most workmen comply but a few get shirty when they turn up early and have to wait. Some have walked off the job when they are reminded that they have an hour to complete their work. Obviously, they have difficulty with the restrictions, and some have said the family is just being awkward. Interestingly, every job card states the time restrictions.

The gentleman also has a problem with medical staff and associates trauma and pain with medical uniforms. One day, a new district nurse turned up at the home unannounced and demanded to see the gentleman. The parents refused entry but not before the gentleman saw the uniform. Later that day, the nurse telephoned and had a go at the parents for 'stopping her doing her duties'. The gentleman's notes clearly state no home visits, especially without notice.

Not listening can also have fatal consequences. Many people may not have heard of Oliver McGowan, but his untimely passing has ensured every medic in the UK has mandatory autism and learning disability training. Mr McGowan tragically died at a tender age having been admitted to hospital where he was given anti-psychotic drugs despite no history of psychosis or mental illness. To learn more about Mr McGowan, please ask your search engine for 'Oliver McGowan story'.

On my journey, the DWP and their subcontractors regularly ignore the notes and contact restrictions, despite their internal procedures. Joe can become situationally mute when using the telephone, especially if it is the DWP, and we are appointees for this reason. DWP Universal Credit officers regularly telephone Joe's mobile about one thing or another and almost always fail to read the notes that state very clearly that we are appointees, and they need to telephone our landline. That said, they are usually officers we don't know face to face. Those we know by sight are much better.

It always amazes me that many expect you and yours to comply with them but won't comply with you, and how angry they get when you remind them of the notes they failed to read.

Education

This is one of the hardest parts of your journey. It will test you beyond your endurance at times, but everything is possible. For example, Joe recently graduated from college and a lady I follow in the USA has two loved ones at MIT studying PhDs. The secret is finding the way that is best for your loved one.

Please remember these guidelines:

- Private isn't always best.
- Zero-tolerance policies are harmful.
- Silly uniform rules are harmful.
- Seclusion booths are harmful.
- Bullies exist.
- Ratings mean nothing.
- The environment is everything.
- LA officers are not your friends.
- Trust your gut over a professional (exceptions apply).

Selecting a school

Unlike many parents who simply select the nearest or catchment school, we need to make an informed choice. This choice may have profound implications for your loved one and may affect their long-term mental health, employability and confidence, or may empower them to achieve beyond your wildest dreams.

When you select a school for your loved one, be mindful of their needs rather than your convenience. Visit the school more than once and take the opportunity of open evenings to visit more than two years beforehand. Ask awkward questions. Understand their policies, especially around behaviour, tolerance and uniforms. If there is no flexibility and little understanding of your loved one's rights or needs as a disabled person, ask yourself if that is the right school.

When we were selecting a senior school, we asked plenty of awkward questions and only one school was transparent. The SENCO (special educational needs coordinator), a remarkable lady affectionally called Mrs C, said they made mistakes but always tried to learn from them. One SENCO in a different school was dismissive when we visited her school a year early. Another had books on autism noticeably placed on her desk.

Many 'better' schools are over-prescribed, but remember a good statutory report doesn't mean a school is the best one for your loved one. Some 'better' schools have zero-tolerance policies on just about everything and will attempt to micromanage your loved one's behaviour. Given your own journey with your loved one, you know that will end badly.

Look at the built environment and look for things that are triggering. Joe didn't like rain when he was little and found the sound of rain on glass roofs unsettling. One of our local senior schools has a glass roof over a central courtyard.

Part of a school environment could include a 'base' where only SEN and disabled students are allowed. Bases provide a haven for vulnerable people. A place where they can unmask and be themselves.

Transitions between schools are important, but it is imperative that your loved one's needs drive the process. Some schools take children on a single short visit to the normal catchment senior school. For Joe, a single short visit would have been insufficient. Additional and specific visits are always required in my opinion. For example, if the school has a base, spend some time there when the other children are present. We were lucky as Joe's primary school TA took him to the senior school on several occasions.

Many schools are businesses nowadays and many appear to exclude readily, and please remember that around 80% of students sent to Pupil Referral Units (PRUs) are autistic (Source GOV.UK, 'Special Educational Needs in England').

Accessing support

Many autistic students need additional support in school. Those needs vary and at times can be complex because of comorbidities.

As your child grows, you will discover additional needs or 'Special Educational Needs' (SEN). These may break either you or your loved one (emotionally and/or mentally). Send Action, a parent SEN group, describes, 'Accessing services for disabled children is like playing a game of pass the bomb'.

One of the most difficult tasks on your journey will be securing and enforcing a Statement of Special Educational Need. In England, these are now known as Educational, Health and Care Plans (EHCP). Acquiring a Statement is dependent on one person: you. Your local authority and perhaps your school may go out of their way to be obstructive. You will hear much about notational £6,000 budgets, initial funding out of the school budget, not reaching an arbitrary threshold etc. They will attempt to blind you with facts and figures and emotionally manipulate you to think of other, less-fortunate children. Some will try a wait-and-see approach, suggesting you try this thing first and then this. Every trick is to delay and save money. Your LA has a finite budget for SEN, but the law doesn't recognise budgets, only need. Obviously, your LA will try to keep all SEN spending within that budget despite how the law is framed.

Some prominent people will state that there are too many SEN children and there is a deluge of EHCPs that are draining school and local authority resources. They will describe a Statement of Special Educational Needs as a 'Golden Ticket', and even discriminatory to non-SEN children. Understand, this is all nonsense and is solely to engender a them-and-us environment. The Public Accounts Committee in the UK Parliament describes this as a false narrative (Parliament, 2020).

John Harris, writing in *The Guardian* (Harris, 2024) says, 'In this imagined reality, sharp-elbowed parents are handed "golden tickets" for endless support. Meanwhile, we battle for the bare minimum.'

These opinions are probably ignorant of the law and the needs of your loved one. Some LA officers will use this approach to make you feel guilty. Remember, your only duty is to your loved one and you don't have to consider the needs of others.

Chapter 3: Practical advice

As you start this journey, the law is your only friend. The IPSEA charity has considerable information on SEN law and regulations. However, some areas of legislation you may find quite helpful are:

Statement/ EHCNA assessment request	CAFA section 36(8)	This should be used by a parent to force an LA to accept a request to assess their loved one for SEN needs.
Issue of a draft EHCP plan	SEND regulation section 13	Some LAs forget that the EHCP/statement processes have statutory timescales.
To properly fund an EHCP	CFA section 42(2) & Hackney HC ruling April 2019	This is used to force a LA to properly fund the required education for a child with special educational needs.
The duty to provide appropriate education	1996 Education Act section 19(1) & (6)	LAs have a duty to provide appropriate education, whether that is mainstream, a special school or a specialist private school.

There are some charities, like IPSEA, and individuals who can help you with the application for an EHCP/statement. On my journey, Mr Gary Freeman, a former SENCO, was helpful with his advice on Twitter and email. If you seek professional help to assist with an EHCP application, go with recommendations from other carers. I personally know Mr Freeman has helped many parents and I have no hesitation in recommending him. Be warned, however, that some people are not what they seem and if they appear too good to be true, they are probably dodgy. For example, locally to us there was a chap who claimed he could get an EHCP in weeks for a price, despite the obvious statutory timescales. Please be aware of the statutory process and timescales, and always hold your LA to them.

There will come a point on this journey when you will have had your fill of excuses and delays. As a parent, you have a right to force your LA to assess your loved one for a Statement of Special Educational Needs using a statutory assessment letter. The IPSEA charity has sample letters you can use.

After Joe was diagnosed, we informed his school and the LA and expected a Statement to follow. After several months, we enquired at the school and learnt they were waiting on the educational psychologist. This was the first time we intervened. Again, nothing happened, but after a forceful push, the psychologist spent two hours talking to us and the SENCO rather than assessing and observing Joe. At the end of the meeting, I remember my partner asking the psychologist how she could find two hours to talk to us but not five minutes for our loved one. A mum crossed is a force of nature and when we returned home, I was instructed to 'go nuclear'. That evening, a statutory assessment request was submitted. We were harangued by the school and LA to withdraw but we continued. I remember a final meeting with the school and Joe's Speech and Language Therapists. The SLTs took charge and finalised a report that stated that there was a need to be met.

The LA rejected the request citing, insufficient need based on a CAHMS report. The CAHMS report said that Joe had difficulty. The LA argued that it didn't prove any difficulty. I recall a conversation with our CAHMS psychologist who intervened on our behalf; she sent a dictionary to the rejecting officer with the word 'difficult' highlighted. The psychologist also resubmitted her report with 'profound' or 'very' in front of every 'difficult' in her report. Our initial rejection helped the psychologist understand why many of her reports were unhelpful. Her reports were 'better received' after that.

Once again, the LA said no. We appealed and decided to go to a tribunal. The LA missed or ignored every deadline. Desperate, I contacted the EHRC to understand where we stood and, luckily, I spoke to a lovely lady who was a secretary to someone important. To cut a long story short, some serious words were said about missing another deadline. As expected, the LA officer ignored the deadline. Shortly after, if my memory serves me correctly, the officer was moved sideways and we got our Statement.

During a meeting with the officer to try and get us to withdraw our request, we were threatened, made to feel guilty, insulted, accused of not understanding autism etc. It is worth noting that the officer deciding the fate of our child had no apparent (to us) relevant qualifications. I vaguely recall the officer was not a teacher, psychologist, doctor or nurse, nor did they hold some other relevant qualification in education or medicine. Always ask whether the officer (or panel) is qualified to say no.

The delay and apparent obstruction are typical. It appears that only blindingly obvious cases go through. One family I know took 11 years to get a Statement for their loved one (a different LA). The family's circumstances meant that the parents didn't always have the energy for a fight. The child had diagnoses of epilepsy, dyslexia, dyscalculia and 'classic' autism and because of the family's circumstances, the parents chose to trust the experts it took 11 years to secure a Statement. In the end, the parents had had enough and asked for a statutory assessment. The Statement followed weeks later.

It must be stated that not all local authorities are this blatantly dismissive or 'exploitative' in using a family's circumstances against them, but some will avoid doing what is morally right to protect their finite budgets[5].

Interestingly, EHCPs contain sections concerned with health and care. Ensure these sections are filled in and are kept up to date. Initially, you may wonder what health and care has got to do with education, but being physically or mentally ill will seriously impact your loved one's education. Remember how you really can't think when you have a heavy cold? If your loved one has anxiety, for example, make sure it is recorded along with recommendations on how to support them.

When Joe was quite unwell, I tried to have his plan amended to include details of the new diagnosis and its impact. The officers I spoke to would not amend the plan as it was only about education, despite me explaining that poor mental health impacts learning. The officers made very good impersonations of two short planks. After many months, the little change was agreed. Luckily, the best SENCO ever, Mrs C, listened and amended the plan herself. Mrs C made a profound difference to the recovery of Joe while the LA seemingly couldn't care any less.

When Joe finished school, I recall a final face-to-face conversation with Mrs C where she said Joe would no longer meet the bar for an EHCP because the LA would expect Joe to cope. I was flabbergasted but not in the least surprised.

Moving home is stressful for most people, but it has an extra hurdle for parents moving across a local authority boundary. The law expects that

---

5   Please remember, there is no correlation between a good LA and the political colour of that authority.

a Statement or EHCP agreed with one authority is accepted by the next. However, the usual nonsense can be expected unless you remind them forcefully of the law.

For EHCPs to work, they must be regularly reviewed and updated to reflect the current needs of your loved one. Treat them as a living document and ensure the reviews happen. During Joe's time in secondary school, a representative of my LA failed to attend any reviews. We always requested their presence and were always insistent at important transition points but were always ignored. I even spoke to the 'head of service' about it.

Many 'SEND' experts on social media and TV will argue that an EHCP should only be given to those with profound needs. Personally, I think that every child with an autism, ADHD etc diagnosis (even suspected) should automatically qualify for an EHCP.

Given the rollercoaster nature of each condition, a child can't wait six months to two years for you to fight the LA. People, especially professionals, forget how dynamic autism is and a child who is coping today could be seriously self-harming the next day. Every autistic child needs an EHCP or Statement. This is a hill I will die fighting on, and I will not yield.

Forms

Forms are the bane of any carer's life – a necessary but bureaucratic nightmare. Every form comes with 'guidance' on how to fill them in. They always speak of your average day and encourage you to describe things as if your life was normal or the same as everyone else's.

When completing forms, you need to be truthful but brutal. Ask yourself how a KGB officer might fill the form in. Use negative words and expressive adjectives. For example, if your loved one struggles with something, it is not *'difficult'* it is *'very difficult'*. Always repeat yourself to reinforce the message.

Also remember to be precise in your choice of descriptive words and decorate wherever possible. A recent encounter with a DWP assessor focused on the word 'carer'. The officer couldn't understand that we are carers. The assessor believed that all carers get paid. With hindsight, I should have decorated *carer* to become *unpaid carer*.

Some forms become legal documents, like statements of educational needs. These documents define the needs, support and accommodations your loved one needs. Always ensure that open-ended commitments or simple desires are avoided because they provide perfect loopholes for others to also benefit from your loved one's funding. Moreover, they enable teachers and your LA to avoid doing anything helpful. They are simply document padding with no legal consequence.

Phrases like 'May benefit from…', 'As required…', 'When staff are available…', 'When necessary…' etc are not enforceable. Choose sentences that quantify, and use '*must*' and '*will*' with quantities as they are far better and are legally enforceable. Leave nothing to your LA's or school's discretion.

Let's imagine for a moment that a Statement was an employment contract. If your employment contract included a line '…may have access to a salary', do you know when and by how much you will be paid? If the contract included the line '…may benefit from holidays', ask whether you are likely to get any and, if so, whether they would be convenient for you… If the contract says 'will need equipment', ask yourself who will provide it and what exactly it would be.

School environment and culture

A school environment is more than just the physical buildings. It can include:

- the smell
- the lighting
- the rules and their enforcement
- the uniform
- the culture
- how bullies are dealt with
- the language staff use
- the training of staff

All of these are linked and may contribute to making school a toxic environment for our loved ones.

I asked some carers I know, and also any carer followers on Twitter, for some examples of the consequences of the silly and petty rules they had encountered. What they had to say illustrates how ignorant many schools are about the law and autism. Schools often claim that 'Uniform is in place for everyone, and we have the same high expectations from all children to look smart and presentable at all times'. The trouble is, however, when someone has sensory issues or is just uncomfortable because of their clothes, how are they supposed to concentrate, let alone work?

One example concerns an autistic young lady who can't wear hard shoes. The school insists on black tights and hard shoes. This young lady wore black socks with her tights, so she was cushioned from the hard shoes to help with her sensory issues. The school bans trainers and socks with tights. After an email explanation, the school 'relaxed' the restriction.

Some (anonymous) parents said the following:

> *'Colour – yes, colour – of headband our ND 7yo needed to wear to feel confident. Hers was blue, the school colour was not blue. She wore full uniform apart from that. Now she doesn't wear uniform at all – thankfully they started to listen. Shouldn't take a fight.'*

> *'My son can't wear hard shoes. So it's a constant fight. Also, can't fasten top buttons against his neck. As usual school say it's uniform policy.'*

Another anonymous parent stated, 'Our daughters were "forbidden" from wearing a hoody because it makes autistic kids hide'. Anecdotally, hoodies are really good at reducing sensory issues and rejecting that explanation clearly shows their ignorance of autism.

The rigidity of the rules and their application is a profound challenge for those with a Pathological Demand Avoidance (PDA) profile. Obviously, when coupled with sensory issues, demand avoidance of the PDA kind makes for all kinds of difficulties.

When I struggle in an office due to a pending migraine, I wear sunglasses and a peak cap, and no one bats an eye. So, is it better that compliance is enforced by demanding that everyone 'do as we say' rather than supporting someone to learn better? An example of the importance of comfort clothing can be found on YouTube[6].

Apart from silly uniform policies, schools nowadays have zero-tolerance policies over behaviour and absence. Many forget that these policies originate in the minds of behaviourists. You may recall that behaviourists push ABA and PBS therapies that are scientifically proven to cause clinical damage to autistic people. These policies appear to assume guilt rather than innocence and the sanctions are totally unjust in comparison with the alleged policy infraction. Many of the rules are contradictory and petty and some of the sanctions are prejudicial to the well-being of many children, let alone autistic or ADHD children. In my opinion, these policies are probably in breach of the law.

> One head teacher picked on Joe because of the school's 'no hands in pockets' policy. A sensory toy was always concealed in a trouser pocket to comply with another contradictory rule. The toy never *distracted* Joe from learning or listening to the teaching staff. On the contrary, it helped to manage his anxiety and thereby enabled learning and considerably reduced any disruption. The constant attention of the head impacted Joe considerably and we needed CAHMS to work through the trauma. A complaint to the SENCO ensured the head's attention was diverted elsewhere.

Many people forget or are ignorant of why sensory toys are useful. I asked the opinion of other carers what they thought schools would do if their loved ones had one of these. Several reported that their loved one's school accepted them as a useful tool in helping their loved one self-regulate and obviously learn with less toxic stress and disruption to the learning of others. Many reported that their loved one's school would automatically confiscate the toys, and many would apply sanctions.

One of those who responded said: 'My nephew had to have his sensory toys written into his IEP to stop the teacher from taking them from him

---

6   www.youtube.com/watch?v = 4Xtog_zRRJg. 'Vanish/Ambitious about Autism: Me, My Autism & I'. The video follows an autistic girl's school day.

anytime she saw him with one, and she still takes it any time he touches one during a lesson. We've tried to explain many times, but she just doesn't get it.'

Another respondent said, 'Well my daughter was given them by teachers then punished for having them. Usually told off missed break or a phone call to me complaining.'

An overlooked issue here is that teachers often give contradictory instructions which cause confusion. For example, an autistic child had an outdoor PE lesson with two teachers. One teacher instructed the child to 'stay there' and the other teacher instructed the child to 'fetch some equipment'. The first teacher told the child off for 'wandering off' and a little later the second teacher chastised the child for not fetching the equipment. The child went from Defcon 3 to 1 in a moment and vehemently objected. The child got secluded for being disrespectful. The usual arguments followed, and it was the child's fault, apparently, for not listening and explaining.

Despite what any school says, bullying exists and autistic people usually make easy targets because of their noticeable differences and lack of a peer support group. There are many anecdotal stories of autistic people being suspended or expelled from school for responding to a bully or having to change schools because of a bully. The costs to your loved one are huge in comparison to those of the bully.

Joe's senior school had a base where only autistic (or suspected) students could go during breaks or when they were in danger of overload. Non-autistic students were forbidden. It provided a haven for Joe. Every school should have a base, and it is a simple reasonable adjustment.

Some carers have ensured their loved ones have been able to defend themselves. A while ago there was a documentary about Luke Jackson, a chap with Asperger Syndrome, who learnt a martial art. (Mr Jackson also wrote a book, *Geeks, Freaks and Aspergers*, and this was one of the first helpful books we bought.)

A friend of mine has two autistic loved ones. Both children were 'fine' as far as their schools were concerned, but both disintegrated as soon as they were home. The endless trauma has long-term consequences. One of the children developed an eating disorder that ultimately hospitalised them as it threatened their very existence. The smell of the school canteen was triggering, but because of school indifference, no allowances or adjustments were made. The other child went selectively mute and endured constant shutdowns and meltdowns.

Another friend's loved one endured school and suffered daily panic attacks, and was often physically sick because of the stress and toxic environment. There have been no instances of sickness or panic attacks since leaving school. Again, the LA and school were not interested in being part of a solution to ensure this child got the education they were legally entitled to.

> When Joe started senior school, his anxiety was so great that he was physically sick. The worry of having to do schoolwork at home and managing to do it in an organised and timely manner was ultimately the cause. Moreover, homework is schoolwork, and therefore it should logically be done in school. Luckily, the school had a homework club, and we were able to employ a private tutor for a few hours a week to also help with homework.

If this sounds like your experience, ask yourself what the continuing trauma will do to your child. On our journey, we were lucky to have a senior school that listened to us and we to them, but this was only possible because of Mrs C, a very formidable lady who just got autism. Despite the efforts of Mrs C, some teachers have left Joe with lifelong trauma. Sadly, not everyone has access to a Mrs C, so all that is left is homeschooling, or home education as some prefer to call it.

If you encounter issues with school policies, please remember that section 6 of the Equality Act (2010) is your friend. This is discussed elsewhere.

Homeschooling

Please be aware that you have a duty to educate your loved one. Some will understand this as a duty to make your child go to school no matter what and will argue quite forcefully that you (as a parent) are to blame for non-attendance. Sadly, many people with these views are teachers.

However, that there are also laws that say you have a duty to care for your loved one. In my opinion, these laws trump the assumptions that your child must be in school. I always ask what a child will learn if their mental state is traumatised by an environment. Are they simply being punished for being ill? What learning takes place in an isolation room? In my opinion, mental health always comes before grades and attendance.

A recent study, by Connolly *et al* (2023), suggests that about 92% of children with school attendance issues are neuro-divergent, and about 84% are autistic. These figures suggest that something fundamentally needs to change in education to accommodate the needs of our loved ones. While it is unlikely that anything meaningful will change in the very near future, ask what you can do to support the learning of your loved one.

Homeschooling, or 'elective home education' as the DfE calls it, requires considerable effort on your part, but it can reduce the burden on your loved one of forcing them to attend school. The reasons for homeschooling/education are complex but should always be driven by the needs of your loved one.

Sadly, some parents feel pressured by some LAs to homeschool to avoid prosecution for non-attendance at school. This is your decision and yours alone, and it is important to understand the consequences of this decision:

- The LA will no longer have a legal duty to secure any of the provisions in a Statement or EHCP.
- The LA will have to review any statement annually.
- The LA 'should' fund SEN support.
- The LA can fund the outside-of-school education under EOTAS regulations.
- The LA can fund SEN support through a personal budget using the direct payment mechanism.

There are many homeschool parent networks and it is worth joining a few before you go down this route. You will need to understand the process and duties that will apply.

There are also schools that provide education online at a cost. The UK government does not provide any financial assistance to help with the funding of homeschooling/education. It may be worth talking to your LA as they may have some resources that may be helpful. Using direct payments means the LA has effectively outsourced its duties to you.

There are a few alternatives, however. Before you formally elect to homeschool, please consider EOTAS or 'Education other than at school'. This approach has been successful for many students who find school a toxic environment for their loved one. This approach is covered by section 61 of the Children and Families Act (2014) and sections 6 and 19 of the Education Act (1996). Using this route, it is possible to fund your loved one's education through a personal budget funded by direct payments from your LA.

Personal budgets and direct payments are discussed in Chapter 9 of the 'SEN and disability code of practice', supported by SEN Regulations (2014). Please seek advice so you understand all the wrinkles in this approach.

Expect the usual fight with your LA if you exercise these rights and add them to the Statement.

If you opt to educate at home, you may find focusing study around your loved one's special interests helpful. A lady I follow on Twitter has successfully used this approach with EOTAS funding with her son (he has an interest in power generation). Recently, he was offered work experience with National Grid.

Examinations

GCSEs and A-levels (UK public examinations at 16 and 18 years of age respectively) are very stressful times for most people, let alone young people with autism. From my experience, I have a few observations that may be helpful:

- Nagging constantly about revision doesn't help, but methodical and appropriate support does.
- Comfort food helps. Chocolate worked for us.

- Downtime is important.
- Planning is important.
- Bite-size revision works.
- Incentives may help but this depends on your child.
- Fewer exams are better.

Your loved one's school will expect and probably demand that your loved one has a totally filled lesson calendar. That only adds stress and increases their burden. A simple reasonable adjustment is to lighten the load for better outcomes. It may be a fight to get the school and LA on side. The reasonable adjustment is to lighten the load for better outcomes.

Joe was allowed to drop two or more subjects after considerable lobbying by us and his SENCO, Mrs C. We argued that less means more, that is, that better results or outcomes in the remaining subjects was preferable. If you think about it logically, it is better for everyone. The school has better stats, and your loved one is happier. Initially, the year head said that the 'free' periods would be used for playing games etc. They were used for needed downtime and to do homework and study. It was something Mrs C ensured happened.

Please keep in mind the issue of masking, and how it relates to someone appearing to cope. An *appearance* of coping doesn't mean that your loved one is coping, so please ensure you push for fewer subjects to ensure they have spare bandwidth to deal with the stress.

BTECs provide an exam-free alternative to A-levels and other qualifications in the UK. 'Exam-free' doesn't mean a loss of rigour, however, and they are probably harder because of the extra work and consistency required to achieve a good grade. There are different levels of BTEC, with level 3 being A-level, level 4 an HNC, and level 5 an HND or foundation degree.

Your local authority has a duty to provide impartial advice on SEN, tribunals and local non-local authority services. Sendias provides impartial advice on SEN matters and Sendist provides similar advice for tribunals. The 'local offer' provides information on those important services. Don't expect the local offer to be up to date or relevant and you may find Google more helpful.

Post-school education

Post-school education is complicated, and you need to remember that your loved one's Statement or EHCP may be invalid in getting additional support for your loved one. The level of the resulting qualification determines whether the Statement or EHCP can be used; HNC or above courses are excluded.

Support has to be reapplied for via the appropriate home nation government. In England, applications are made through Student Finance England. Disabled Student Allowance (DSA) provides equipment, some academic support, and perhaps some transport.

Healthcare

One of the most important aspects of this journey is understanding and working with people in health care. Some of these people will test you, while many others will surprise you. This section applies equally to both you and your loved one.

In the UK, most health care is provided by our NHS. The NHS is devolved, and services will vary by home country and by region. Most people imagine a health system operates as a monolith, but it is a web of different and sometimes overlapping commissioned services. Some services will be provided by third parties, including charities and businesses, local authorities, and general hospitals. All services and their access pathways (and triage criteria) will be commissioned and decided by Care Commissioning Groups, Integrated Care Boards or Area Health Boards. Different pathways can sometimes end at the same service.

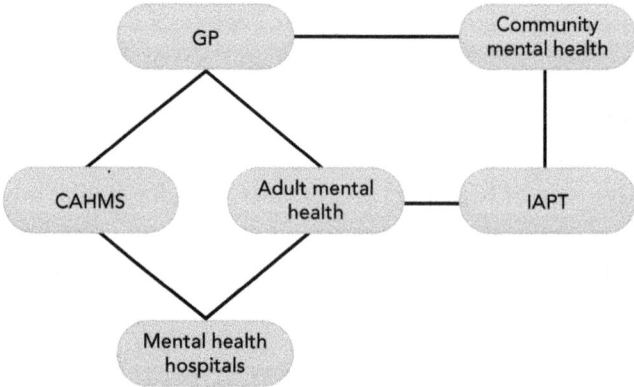

The connections between services can appear to be daunting to clinicians as well as ordinary people. The figure on p.126 shows a very simplistic overview of mental health services.

To access any service in a timely manner, it pays to understand some of this complexity, so the most appropriate pathway can be selected. This is especially true when many people, including clinicians, prioritise physical health over mental health, but both are intertwined, and a mental health condition or illness can manifest through physical symptoms.

It is rare that individual healthcare professionals, healthcare organisations and policymakers work cooperatively to support your loved one. The only person who can ensure less inequality and better medical outcomes is you, as you advocate and badger to improve healthcare quality and access for your loved one.

Communication

Most of the challenges you will face originate in poor communication, assumptions, and the intertwining of physical and mental health. Most medical systems are geared for physical health, and most have little understanding of autism (although that is slowly changing). Accessing physical and mental health support and services can be problematic for many autistic people and their carers.

You are probably aware that autistic people have considerable health inequality and the stark facts of the matter is that many can die up to 12 years earlier than their peers, with suicide being one of the most prominent causes (Sharpe, 2019). Autistic people are socially disadvantaged and often 'hidden' from existing health and social care services. Poor communication exacerbates this situation and can have unexpected consequences.

All communication is a two-way street and poor communication can result from the assumptions and biases of clinicians and their lack of exposure to autism. Poor communication can also result from clinicians and others failing to pass on or discarding relevant information. For example, during one visit to A&E a receptionist forgot to inform the triage team that Joe was autistic.

Effective communication is paramount, but how do you ensure it is effective? This is hard to quantify without knowing you, but the following may be helpful:

- Be firm and loud.
- Constantly remind them about autism.
- Always have a sunflower lanyard to hand.
- Have a 'Patient Passport'.
- Have a laminated A5 card stating basic needs and sensory issues.
- Remember you are the expert.
- Always ask why.
- Be prepared to endlessly repeat the story.
- 'Translate' for clinicians.
- Demand copies of every referral.
- Always advocate.
- Get medical Power of Attorney (POA) or Guardianship if appropriate.

Gatekeepers

Gatekeepers abound in the medical world. Expect to be excluded for a range of reasons that usually come down to ignorance, blame and discrimination. Some will simply blame autism to exclude, others will say your loved one is not disabled enough, and others will simply discriminate.

On our journey, we have been denied access to CAHMS 'because all autistic people have anxiety', and told our loved one was not disabled because 'there is no physical evidence of a disability'. Other gatekeepers/receptionists have failed to pass on important information that would have prioritised Joe.

If you encounter a defiant gatekeeper, my best advice is to go around them. For example, when we were denied access to CAHMS, we wrote to the appropriate manager. Another time we were waiting in A&E for a triage. Every plea with the receptionist/gatekeeper met with indifference. By chance, I caught the eye of the triage nurse and just asked for an idea of how long we would have to continue to wait. The nurse prioritised Joe when she learnt Joe was autistic and on the verge of DEFCON 1.

Many clinicians and some parents forget that autistic people feel pain and discomfort quite differently from most. Both can be less or more intense. When your loved one informs you of a medical issue, there is a rapidly closing window of opportunity for you to act before anxiety makes the task of accessing help very difficult. Sadly, many medical gatekeepers are unaware of this aspect of autism and may not offer a timely solution or appointment. Luckily, my GP surgery has improved and will, where possible, offer a same-day appointment, and when it can't, it prioritises access to our local walk-in centre. A walk-in centre is like A&E but provides GP-level services. Luckily, they appear to get autism. Our walk-in centre is responsive if you mention autism and where you are with managing the expectant anxiety.

Support for carers of adults is rare. Parents are generally able to stay on or near children's wards, but usually there is nothing for carers of autistic adults. Many carers report medics may not understand why they need to be constantly present. Many medics rigorously enforce visiting hours and rules. Those who have been accommodated report having to sleep on the floor, eat in the on-site Costa and wash in the public toilets. Some medical staff appear to totally ignore carers despite their detailed knowledge of their loved ones.

> Our friend's loved one had to be admitted for a week in a burns unit following a scalding accident. This child is non-verbal with profound learning disabilities. The senior doctors deferred to our friend's knowledge of his loved one, but junior doctors and nurses did not. My friend asked them to leave his loved one to sleep, but rules are rules. His loved one was regularly woken at 2:00am for a temperature reading and at 6:30 for breakfast. The nursing staff didn't understand the near-constant state of meltdown and why being left to sleep was the best policy. My friend was scolded for giving his loved one crisps and sweets. My friend's attitude was that any food is better than none, and comfort food is always guaranteed to be eaten.

How can you avoid this? Some people have suggested that a medical passport is the way to go. Suitable template passports can be downloaded from the NAS and the NHS websites. Others have suggested attaching a list of primary needs to the medical doors or room door. It is worth reminding staff of their mandatory autism training and to read the medical passport and the notes on the door. It may be an idea to summarise the medical passport and attach the summary to your loved one's hospital passport or end-of-bed notes.

Dentists are disliked by most people for one reason or another. However, we all know that regular check-ups keep teeth healthy. Dentists are full of sensory hell, from overly bright lights, cold tools, vacuum pumps that suck the water from your soul, drills and people who need to touch a very sensitive area. How do you manage the dentist or the hygienist?

On our journey, hygienists appear to be the least patient or accepting people on the planet. Dentists have been more accepting and willing to change their practice to help. According to my dentist, they receive very limited training on SEN etc. My advice is to talk to your dentist beforehand, and you will be surprised how flexible they can be.

Environment

Most medical and dental facilities are not ideal for autistic people. Usually, they are bright, very noisy, busy, and almost guaranteed to result in sensory overload. The issues are complex and, as expected, are different for each autistic person. We have found familiarity, immediacy, or set appointments helpful.

Accidents and emergencies (A&E) or emergency rooms are not ideal environments for autistic people. Usually, the lights are too bright, the chairs are uncomfortable, the vending machines buzz and the TVs blast out the news. Most A&Es have no means of informing you of your position in the waiting-to-be-triaged or waiting-to-be-seen queues. For Joe, a leader board with expected wait times would be helpful as it is easier to manage pain and anxiety when you know how long you may have to wait.

Some A&Es have a quiet room. Our local A&E has one, but it is now obviously the overflow area. Previously, it was a storage space.

Other carers and autistic people have said overnight hospital stays are difficult. Many have said large wards and the overwhelming noise and brightness pushes them to overload very easily. Many have said a private room with some autonomy would be ideal, and nothing should happen unexpectedly. For example, a porter appearing to collect your loved one for an unexpected x-ray is problematic. Many recommend having a laminated sign on the room door or entrance explaining or stating that the occupant is autistic, and perhaps listing their most important needs, such as for quiet or for low lighting. Many suggest a transition and a story for autistic children. For many, the lack of privacy is a problem and the absolute loss of autonomy and disregard of specific needs. For example, others making decisions about you without you and not respecting your boundaries, like always being warned of events during the day.

If you have a scheduled appointment, it may be worth visiting the location initially to know where you need to go, to locate the parking, the toilets etc. Preparing and planning will make it more bearable for you, and obviously for your loved one.

Prevention

One of the simplest 'benefits' you can do is to register yourself and your partner, if you have one, as carers, and register your loved one as autistic with your GP. While this may not prioritise access to your GP, it might help. It makes a small difference with my GP, and they appear to be more flexible. Registering ensures you are included in any vaccination programmes earlier than your age would normally allow.

We have taken a preventative approach with yearly check-ups. Joe has an electric toothbrush and an electric water-based flosser. The flosser has reduced the need for a hygienist. We remind our dentist about autism, what not to do and why it shouldn't be done.

Mental health

I recently watched a TED talk featuring an autistic lady. She was happily married, had a lovely home, a successful career following university. She went to see her GP who said she had a perfect life, and then that straw broke the camel's back. Through tears and considerable anguish, she explained how exhausting her life was from endless masking, how every day was becoming an increasing struggle and yet no one noticed. They pushed for more joy and smiles and conformity but didn't notice the cracks, the near-fatal tears. They nearly learnt the hardest lesson of all.

This is the hardest part of this journey. As you have learnt, autism is complex and the bundle of interactions can make life interesting. Autistic people have a difficult relationship with mental health. Simon explains it succinctly: 'A giant chunk of it is probably because we have to pay rent on our right to exist'.

Accessing mental health services is difficult for autistic people. The reasons are complex and include historical and cultural themes and clinical assumptions. Brede *et al* (2022) were part of a large survey of mental health services and reported, 'Our findings show that currently, mental health services do not adequately support autistic adults, and can even cause additional harm'.

Based on the journey of many families, the issues are simple:

- Triage and *urgency*.
- Sizing and appropriateness of services.
- Harm.

Triage or gatekeeping is a big one and is linked with urgency. Many physical health issues, like a broken arm or a heart attack, result in almost immediate treatment, and follow-up appointments are arranged. In contrast, mental health issues (and diagnosis) are not met with the same urgency. You may recall the story of the lady who had to be 'abandoned' by her family. Catharine Fairbairn, a carer, explains, 'I've watched loved ones suffer with serious physical illness and serious mental illness. The physical illness was a sideshow compared to the suffering, isolation and lack of support for the person in mental distress.'

Some clinicians may cause harm. Remember the 2000 souls detained under the MHA? When Joe needed help years ago, he saw a CBT therapist who abandoned him after one session. The service decided they couldn't help by blaming autism. Joe got worse.

Prof Rodgers (2022) explored the barriers to accessing support and concluded that much is down to a lack of access, historical underfunding, and a lack of training and consensus on how to best support autistic people.

Many people forget bad mental health can have serious consequences for physical health.

You have probably realised that dealing with mental health issues needs professional help, however accessing that support requires resilience, perseverance and research. Remember, the importance of lived experience and timely intervention.

There are some little changes you can do to support. We take a low-arousal approach to life, for example, if Joe has masked, we encourage downtime. We avoid unnecessary confrontations and use kinder words. We try to avoid social isolation by taking Joe to meet his friends and volunteering, and quietly arranging meetups and activities with other carers. Our most effective support is 'Magic Emma', a clinical psychologist who supports Joe weekly. Emma has lived experience.

We know best

This journey has taught me that medical staff don't always know best, and they almost certainly don't know your loved one. Some won't have read anything but the briefest of skims before talking to you. Moreover, when they don't listen mistakes are made (think of Oliver McGowan), so be insistent and assertive, and having to tell the whole negative story again takes up valuable time.

A probably autistic elderly relative's needs were totally disregarded. Even when I suggested that they remember my relative was probably autistic and they should discuss and plan things beforehand, the request was ignored. I was given the impression they knew best, and any suggestions were classed as interference.

To work around this, we always try to see the same doctor. Familiarity also helps, as Joe takes a while to be comfortable around strangers. Our preferred GP usually has overrunning appointments, so we take a distraction or two to manage the expected wait. The surgery appears to be adapting and appears to occasionally bump Joe up the queue when it gets too stressful. Recently, our alternative GP saw Joe when our preferred GP was running very late. That simple intervention saved a lot of anxiety.

Sometimes, clinicians fail to see the link between certain symptoms and autism. Some of these clinicians accuse the parents and child of making an illness up if they can see no supporting evidence. Accusations of a fabricated illness are sticky. Many people will believe a clinician over a parent and child. Many years later, the 'fabricated illness' has been explained following an autism diagnosis. If you are ever accused of fabricating an illness, please remind the clinician that autistic people feel pain and discomfort and the world totally differently to average folk, and that their symptoms may not present in the same way.

The law and knowing your rights

This section describes how autistic people are seen and not seen. It is imperative that your loved one understands their rights. This is especially true when the police are involved.

Equality and discrimination

The Equality Act (2010) is your friend. It is worth familiarising yourself with the statutory guidance. Section 6 defines a disability as an impairment that has long-term and substantial effects on someone's ability to carry out normal day-to-day activities. A diagnosis is not necessary. There are five types of discrimination: direct, indirect, disability, failure to make reasonable adjustments and harassment/victimisation.

Exclusion is an example of direct discrimination, for example if your child is stopped going on a school trip because staff think they won't be able to join in.

Indirect discrimination is probably a bit more complex. You may recall the story of an invigilator forcing Joe to sit until the end of an exam despite overheating. In a mixed examination with students with and without extra time, those without extra time are usually allowed to leave rather than wait for those with extra time to finish.

Disability discrimination occurs when someone is treated unfavourably because of their disability. In a moment you will read about an incident involving Joe and a police officer on a train. Joe produced proof that he was autistic, but the officer continued to 'question' him. The question is, did the officer treat Joe unfairly?

You may recall the story of the head with zero tolerance for hands in pockets. This is probably an example of a failure to make a reasonable adjustment.

You may recall the discussion about sticky labels. A teacher using a sticky label to describe an autistic child in class is probably victimising the child.

This act has been a godsend when dealing with issues where you feel like you are banging your head against a brick wall. Obviously, you need to tie the relevant parts of the act to the points you wish to make. For example, when Joe was ill several years ago, I suggested our NHS was discriminating against Joe because they used autism as an excuse not to refer. Shortly after, we were able to access appropriate support.

Police

Autistic people are vulnerable (Section 2, Protection of Vulnerable Adults Regulations 2002). This is important because interactions with police officers can have long-term impacts on an autistic person.

> Before and during the pandemic, Joe commuted to college by train on his own. This was a huge milestone. On Joe's last unaccompanied journey, he was 'questioned' by a Transport Police officer because he wasn't wearing a face mask for sensory reasons. Despite Joe having a sunflower lanyard and a government ID card, he was not believed. You may remember autistic people were exempt. The consequences of that brief encounter are still with us today.

Police have a statutory duty to make reasonable adjustments to how they interact with vulnerable people (PACE Code C 2019). This duty includes the provision of an appropriate adult (AA) to ensure the vulnerable person's rights are respected, the person understands what is happening to them, to ensure their welfare is considered, and reasonable adjustments are made. Given the naivety of some autistic people and their capacity to overshare, it is sometimes easy to manipulate them into making false statements. The appropriate adult is there to safeguard against this. An appropriate adult is different to a solicitor and is not there to offer legal advice.

The National Appropriate Adult Network (NAAN, 2024) reports that, 'Previous studies have indicated that as many as 39% of adults in police custody have a mental disorder or intellectual disability' and that 'There were large variations, particularly in voluntary interviews, as different police forces recorded rates of AA need between 0% to 24%'. This issue is discussed in greater detail in the NAAN Report, *There to Help 2*, (Bath, 2019).

I understand that police officers have a lot to deal with and, culturally, we expect a lot of them. So how do we ensure autistic people receive the support they are legally entitled to?

Let's consider it from a police officer's point of view for a moment. As we know, autism is invisible, it can be difficult for even an experienced police officer to notice that a person is autistic and, without lived experience, many may not understand the implications of a meltdown or shutdown.

The officer may not understand the consequences of that social-justice trait or how a non-verbal or situationally mute person may appear uncooperative. In each of these scenarios, an officer may make the wrong assumptions and make any distress considerably worse.

Despite Joe's encounter, we occasionally remind him of his rights and of the need to inform anyone in an official capacity that he is autistic. Anecdotally, many autistic people have said they are simply not believed. Some police forces have acted to change this and operate schemes whereby vulnerable people can register so they are hopefully treated better. These schemes are local in nature.

To ensure an appropriate adult is present, your loved one needs to repeatedly identify themselves as autistic. Some autistic people will caution against such declarations as they distrust the police and authority. They believe it will ensure they are treated badly and that the police should know they are vulnerable.

Police have short-term detention powers under the Mental Health Act, and some autistic people have been arrested when in a state of distress. It is imperative that, if your loved one is distressed, they contact you or a friend immediately to ensure section 135/136 detentions are avoided.

Police have statutory powers to stop and search anyone. A 'stop and search' request by a police officer may be triggering for some autistic people. People stopped are expected to cooperate, but this may be problematic for autistic people given their probable strong sense of social justice and communication difficulties. It is also possible that the officer decided the person looked suspicious because of a stim, a shutdown or a meltdown. A police officer may wrongly assume that the person is uncooperative. Your loved one should inform the officers that they are autistic if possible and always ask to see the officer's warrant card.

Autistic witnesses face similar hurdles as suspects. Every police force has specialist officers who are trained in interviewing autistic people. Their main priority will always be to keep your loved one safe and to preserve any evidence. The police are generally quite flexible and will allow your loved one to be supported by a carer, a relative or an advocate. They can also provide a registered intermediary to assist officers. If an adjustment is needed simply ask.

Courts

Autistic people are more likely to be victims of crime than perpetrators. When an autistic person commits an offence, it may be due to one or more of the following reasons:

- Social naivety.
- Difficulty with unexpected change.
- Misunderstanding social cues.
- Others simply not understanding autism.

Many autistic people may not be as 'street-wise' as their peers and their naivety may make them easy targets for criminals who befriend them and use them as unwitting accomplices.

As you know, change can be difficult and triggering, and many may see the consequent behaviour as unacceptable. Some may 'push your loved one's buttons' deliberately. Some may automatically class their behaviour as anti-social.

Misunderstanding social cues is autism 101, and sadly many people don't get this, and the consequences can be catastrophic… Imagine if an autistic person misinterprets someone's flirting?

Rules are rules, and that black-and-white autistic approach could be troublesome when some discretion is required. For example, a delivery driver parking in a disabled spot may get his tyres kicked.

Obviously, some of these examples are trivial but if the behaviour doesn't change charges may follow.

Some autistic people may be unable to enter a plea if any charges get to court. Lawyers and judges can ask for psychiatric reports to determine whether a person is fit to enter a plea. It is essential that any reports are written by someone who specialises in autism. A judge can order a 28-day detention for an autistic defendant to be assessed in a local mental health unit.

A 'Registered Intermediary' may be necessary to help court officials phrase questions for an autistic person. This is usually at a judge's discretion.

Recent research from Cambridge University (Slavny-Cross *et al*, 2022) suggests that trials of autistic people may be unfair. In nearly 50%

of jury trials, the jury was not informed the defendant was autistic. Moreover, nearly 60% of prosecution barristers and 50% of judges said or did something that suggested they had an inadequate understanding of autism. In addition, a significant number of defendants received no reasonable adjustments or support. These factors alone leave a defendant at a considerable disadvantage, as a jury may interpret atypical responses wrongly. For example, a lack of eye contact could be interpreted as a sign of lying. Similarly, a judge may fail to take into consideration mitigating factors that might otherwise influence sentencing. That said, 60% of judges accept autism as a mitigating factor.

Autistic witnesses face similar issues to autistic defendants. Without guidance, a jury may misinterpret the atypical behaviour of a witness. However, that said, the judge and police have considerable discretion in making being a witness as stress free as possible. Adjustments can include screens, pre-recorded testimony, use of aids, a registered intermediary, clearing the court and no formal court attire like wigs.

Mental Health Act and suicide

This is an open sore for the autistic community. The current UK Mental Health Act (1983) – or MHA – classes autism as a mental illness/disorder. Most informed people know that autism is not and never has been a mental health illness. That said, autistic people can develop a mental illness because of how society treats them.

The Mental Health Act contains several pathways to detention, each with different legal rights. Most people are sectioned under sections 2, 3 and 5. Section two is used to detain someone for their own health or safety or the safety of others. Section two allows detention for a maximum time of 28 days while waiting for an assessment. This period cannot be extended, although a clinician can decide to detain someone for longer under section 3. Under section 3, a person can be detained in six-month blocks, up to a year, and can then be held indefinitely. Section 5 applies to voluntary patients and gives a mental health nurse the power of detention. Time limits apply to section 5.

Sections 135 and 136 give the police the power to detain you for a day. A warrant is required to detain you under section 135. Section 136 gives a police officer the power to detain you if you appear to have a mental disorder and are 'in need of care or immediate control'. The period can be extended to 36 hours. Consider how a sensory overload or meltdown may appear to an untrained police officer, especially if the person is non-compliant or unresponsive. More details of your rights and the timescales can be found at the Equality and Human Rights Commission website[7].

During the winter of 2022, around 2000 plus autistic and learning-disabled (LD) people were detained under the MHA in the UK (Parliament, 2022). The average detention for a non-autistic person was 27 days, but in comparison the average detention for an autistic or LD person was over five years. Many detainees are held in conditions such as solitary confinement, that will ensure they develop mental illnesses.

Many people believe that such detention, without an individualised therapeutic value, violates an individual's Article 5 (of the European Convention on Human Rights) right to liberty and security. Many also believe this violates a considerable portion of the UN Convention on the Rights of Persons with Disabilities (UNCHRPD).

Autistic people are more likely than the average person to have suicidal ideation. Some researchers say this is up to nine times more in adults and 28 times in children, and others that it is significantly higher than the background rate. Autistic suicidal ideation presents very differently from the average. There have been many media reports of sectioned autistic people who have been able to fatally harm themselves while detained.

There have also been reports of autistic people being charged with offences while trying to take their own lives. In early 2023, a young adult female was charged with causing a public nuisance and a 12-year-old girl was charged with criminal damage when she resisted being forcibly restrained. In late 2023, an autistic chap attempted suicide in a Job Centre. He has been charged with a public nuisance offence and being in possession of a lethal chemical (to poison himself).

A few autistic people are classed as repeat offenders after taking themselves to A&E with suicidal ideation. Some NHS Trusts and police forces use Serenity Integrated Mentoring (SIM) to control 'high-intensity' individuals. The approach 'mentors' people not to use the health service.

---

7   www.equalityhumanrights.com/

The approach is widely considered controversial. My local mental health trust has decided not to use SIM because they believe it escalates rather than deescalates. In my opinion, it makes death more likely.

The Mental Health Act can also be a way of ensuring your loved one gets the immediate support they need. A family known to me had tried for years to access mental health support for their loved one. Despite several trips to the 'pit of no return' (attempted suicide), the family was deemed as coping and only when the family 'abandoned' their loved one at A&E (on the quiet advice of a mental health nurse) did they receive appropriate and much-needed help.

The Mental Health Act can be used to detain someone indefinitely. I read about an autistic man who was sentenced to indefinite detention in a hospital under section 37 of the MHA for hacking. The original article was published in *The Guardian* newspaper in December 2023 (Badshah, 2023). The article raises questions about proportionality and professional assumptions about autism.

The main point of this section is that you learn about your loved one's rights and act immediately to protect their liberty while also ensuring their health and safety.

The most important thing you can teach your loved one is to remember to tell those in authority that they are autistic. Remind them that they must never overshare or say anything until an advocate, or you, are present. Moreover, they must always ask for the duty solicitor if cautioned.

Ageing

When your loved one first appears, your own demise is probably the thing furthest from your mind, but it does require considerable thought. As you notice the little differences and get a diagnosis, it is *essential* that you think about what you need to happen at your end of days, or the end of your caring days.

The end of my days is a subject that preoccupies me. It is like that egg timer slowly running down, reminding me of their approach and what I have still to do. We have wills, a discretionary trust, a small second home, and some savings. We have discussed everything with Joe's siblings, but sometimes it feels like I need more time to prepare them for their journey. This obviously assumes they will be able to support Joe.

A few years ago, Joe's PA told me a story of the 'lad that was never known'. A lady in her 80s died and there was apparently no family to organise her funeral and estate, and it was left to the local authority. Much to the local authority's surprise, the lady had left behind an autistic son with learning disabilities. The gentleman was apparently totally unknown to the LA. He was rehoused in supported living with the charity that supports Joe. This raises the question of how joined up are services?

After hearing this story, I asked my adult social care team how this case was possible so I could better plan for my end of days. Apparently, despite being the local registrar, they wait for someone to tell them of your death. There is no link between the registrar and social services. My only advice is to plan as best you can.

My plan

As I have no idea when I will pass or become unable to care for Joe, I have developed a six-point plan that will hopefully enable me to continue to support Joe when I can no longer actually do the task:

- A prepaid funeral with my wishes already known.
- A USB memory stick/backup holding all the important documents relating to Joe and my assets.
- A 'living' document with details of people who will make decisions concerning Joe.
- A safe containing all the appropriate paperwork including my will.
- A 'living' letter explaining everything to Joe.
- Discussing the execution of my estate with the persons I hope will be the executors of my estate.

Please remember, unless your loved one has a PA or support worker, your LA won't step in when you die. You need to plan for this eventuality.

Write a will

The most obvious thing you can do is write a will. Given the vulnerability of your loved one, it is best to seek professional legal advice to consider all your options. Please be mindful to legally safeguard and protect any money or assets you may wish to leave to your loved one.

If you write a will with professional legal advice, ask about trusts and how they can be structured to support your loved one. Remember to pick your trustees with care, as promises made now may not be kept, and make sure your choice of trustees will always act in the best interests of your loved one – and ensure they are younger than you. Trusts can protect your assets from the vagaries of friends, local authorities, and government departments.

You may wonder why a trust is important. Many years ago, I attended a seminar given by an autistic chap who nearly lost his home because of his naivety. He was left his grandmother's house so he would always have a home. A 'friend' encouraged him to sign the house over to her as she would 'look after him'. Luckily, the chap spoke to his siblings before signing the paperwork. The family immediately transferred the home into a trust to protect him. The Land Registry offer a free notification service if there is any change in potential ownership of a property you have an interest in.

If grandparents leave bequests for your loved one, talk to them about having the bequests made in trust to ensure the assets are ring-fenced to ensure they don't affect your loved one's financial position. Always seek legal advice when setting up trusts, to ensure authorities like the DWP don't class the trust as an asset or income.

One of the most difficult decisions you need to make is choosing an executor for your estate. Obviously, while trust is important, the person must also be able to deal with the issues related to your loved one to ensure they are supported and cared for. One of the hardest parts of being an executor is discovering where everything is. Discovery is time-consuming, and the paperwork can be onerous depending on the institution. Having a document listing all assets spares your executor this discovery phase.

A prepaid funeral removes the burden of organising your funeral. The funeral directors will take care of everything. It may be possible for them to deal with many of the funeral-related duties on your behalf.

Paperwork

Having acted as an executor for two loved ones and as a Power of Attorney for another, I can say with authority that having an organised approach to paperwork will make life easier for whoever picks up the baton.

I have three categories of paperwork:

- Medical
- Government/legal
- Personal

One of the most important purchases you can make is an A4 scanner, a shredder, and a network backup disc. The scanner will enable you to keep electronic copies of all important documents. The backup drive will ensure you don't lose anything. It is worth scanning everything and making a backup periodically.

During your journey, you will accumulate quite a lot of medical and government legal paperwork. Given the volume of paperwork, it is worth periodically sanitising it, so expired appointment letters, for example, are discarded. By having scanned copies, it is possible to reduce the storage required without losing any paperwork.

It is important that everything related to diagnoses is collated and put in a safe place. Future social security and social care requests may depend on it. Moreover, certain government paperwork is a prerequisite to accessing some services without confrontation. For example, a Disability Living Allowance (DLA) or Personal Independent Payment (PIP) award letter removes numerous bureaucratic hurdles at a stroke.

My personal paperwork includes two living documents. The first or help document relates to the institutions, people and charities involved in Joe's life. The second is for my loved ones.

The help document contains details of the contact people at my local authority and the charities and trusts that support Joe. The document lists any documentary compliance required to maintain services and an overview of how to fill in certain forms and when an update is next expected. The document also includes bank details to pay for the services we use and are expected to pay for.

As you age it may be difficult to maintain a living help document of contacts. Generally, people may change but the main access points and roles will still exist. For example, local authorities will always have an adult social care team and if you are already registered with them as a carer your loved one should be known to them. A generalised description of their role may be sufficient for your estate's executor. I deal with most of the local authority and government paperwork that relates to Joe. It is imperative that someone else knows what comes from where and how to fill in the appropriate paperwork. For example, if you get a direct payment for a PA from your local authority, you will have to complete some paperwork periodically, so the LA understands that the money is spent appropriately.

The other living documents are simple documents to my children explaining why everything was done the way it was and what each of them meant to me. It is important to remind each one of them how much they will be missed and my regret at not having enough time to dedicate to those without invisible disabilities.

Other things

Many families fall out over the sharing of assets when someone dies. Even with a will, things can still be troublesome especially if there are multiple executors and presumed favouritism. If your loved one lives in the family home, your passing may unintentionally make them homeless following the sale of the home.

Some may see a 'right of abode' as favouritism. Moreover, your loved one may be unable to afford to run the home, given local property taxes, insurance costs and basic utility charges.

Depending on your resources, a simple solution may be to buy a small property for your loved one to live in when you pass. If you do this, it is imperative that you discuss it with your loved one (and their siblings), so they understand you are protecting and not abandoning them. It may be worth putting this dwelling in a trust (make sure you seek appropriate legal advice about trusts).

If you live in a council or social housing, it may be useful to add your loved one to the rental agreement to ensure they are not made homeless when you pass. If they are named on the rental agreement, their tenure is almost guaranteed (subject to contractual terms and conditions etc).

It is important that all those who benefit understand how you have constructed your estate and that they accept and believe it to be fair. You may be reliant on them to advocate and act as trustees for your loved one.

Final thoughts

Grief can be quite different for autistic people and your loved one may not respond as others expect. Some charities provide grief counselling for autistic people. This is something I have added to my 'living' help document.

It may seem obvious, but when picking executors, try to pick people younger than yourself for obvious reasons, and also pick at least two. In addition, consider lasting Powers of Attorney for yourself so that, if you lose capacity, someone can take over.

If you keep a lot of data on your mobile phone, add one of your executors or children as a legacy contact. This will enable them to recover the data from your phone without the need for a court warrant or order.

Employment

Culturally, we define people by what they do, that is, their main job. You may recall my earlier discussion about different hats. As a society, we expect everyone to have a job and generally look down upon those who are unemployed. Most parents hope their children have meaningful work, i.e. work they enjoy doing. Sadly, for carers and our loved ones, life is more complicated.

There are many statistics about the employment issues that many autistic adults and carers face. Autistica, a large UK-based autism charity, says only 30% of autistic people are in work. That said, many autistic people hold down specialised jobs. You hear of autistic teachers, lecturers, doctors and business leaders. These people are exceptional, but there are many who struggle to find meaningful work. Carers UK has similar statistics about unpaid carers (Petrillo *et al*, 2022).

A few years ago, I watched an interview with Tim Cook, CEO of Apple, at the Oxford Foundry (part of the University of Oxford), in which he discussed the success of Apple. He said the most fundamental part of that success was the diversity of the development teams. Diversity in background and diversity in thinking. The thinking part was a very important component of that diversity. Autistic and other neuro-divergent people think differently from many other people. Some are very good at recognising patterns most never see and developing innovative ideas that are from the left field.

In recent years, employers are increasingly realising that embracing neurodiversity, especially autism, offers a competitive advantage. A recent *Harvard Business Review* article reported (Taylor, 2017) that 'Many people with neurological conditions such as autism spectrum disorder and dyslexia have extraordinary skills, including in pattern recognition, memory, and mathematics' and that, 'The work for managers will be harder, but the payoff to companies will be considerable: access to more of their employees' talents, along with diverse perspectives that will help them compete'.

Recruitment agencies

Most employment is found these days through employment agencies. Some agencies are ignorant of or indifferent to equality and discrimination legislation. Anecdotally, some agencies don't forward CVs from openly autistic people because they assume the employers who commissioned them may not be interested. Joe was told by an agent that employers don't like disabled people. That said, however, there are some genuine ones who will listen.

Most agents never inform someone when they have had their application rejected. This limbo land is discourteous and quite disquieting for most people but can be considerably worse for autistic people. There is a danger they may start wondering what is wrong with them. However, as just discussed, some enlightened employers have begun to realise the value of neuro-divergent thinking and the innovation it bring to their companies.

There are some autism -centred recruitment agencies such as Auticon (and to some degree ADHD-centred ones). They generally operate in larger cities and work with more enlightened companies that have realised the benefits of employing autistic people. A few of the larger autism charities, like Autistica and 'Ambitious about Autism' also do a weekly job email posting service listing opportunities with many companies. Occasionally, some of the roles are only open to autistic people.

It is worth reminding agents how productive autistic people are or, as Ludmila Praslova, writing in the *Harvard Business Review* in 2021, puts it, 'Did you know that an autistic professional is up to 140% more productive than an average employee when properly matched to a job that fits their skills'.

Interviews

Several years ago, I interviewed with a large company but did not mention my caring life. Everything was very positive until I met the HR Manager and I mentioned my caring role, at which point the interview went downhill. When I have reapplied there since, I have not even had an email response.

One of the most significant stumbling blocks is the interview process. Face-to-face formal chats may be difficult for many autistic people. In general, having your experience and life scrutinised by three or more strangers can be daunting for most people, especially when you are stuffed into a suit across a brightly lit table. Many interviewers ask open-ended questions, and expect you to justify your basic existence and what you'd bring to their business. While you are doing this, they expect good eye contact, openness and warmth and a commitment to their organisation.

Many employers now ask whether you need any 'reasonable adjustments' when you apply for a role. Anecdotally, if a disability is declared or a reasonable adjustment is requested, many applications may never reach the interview stage. Joe has experienced this. Moreover, given the rise of electronic pre-interview vetting, some applications are rejected within seconds. This happened to Joe when applying to be a trainee barista.

Some interviewers are openly hostile to autistic people. Joe has had an interview abruptly terminated because he 'had not declared his disability'.

I work on a freelance basis and have had more interviews than most people. Lately, many potential employers have been setting competency tests before or during interviews. Many also have set questions they use during interviews. I have noticed that the tests and questions are open rather than closed. Open questions have consequences which include shutdown or oversharing. I personally don't like competency tests as I always like to prepare for tests and open questions. Nowadays, I have taken to asking for them in advance of an interview, but many are reluctant to do this. If I can't have such a reasonable and simple request, how are our loved ones supposed to cope?

Some autistic people have described the interview process to me as a 'hell specifically designed to torment autistic people', and the interview itself as 'opaque social crucibles where you are judged on specific but unclear social rules no one has explained'. Some believe they are judged on appearance and rule-adherence rather than any ability to do the job.[8]

The NAS and employer-focused websites have lots of advice for employers on how to interview autistic people. The sites also have advice for autistic people.

There is little advice I can give other than to be supportive, avoid creating stress and always ask for questions in advance of interviews. Practice the answers to any questions and know your CV inside out.

---

8   Twitter and personal correspondence

Types of working

Nowadays, there appears to be more choice in the type of work or ways of working we can expect, as emphasis has shifted to improve well-being and work-life balances. There are part-time, zero-hours, full-time, freelance, self-employed, volunteering, site-based, hybrid and fully remote roles in some companies. The flexibility helps employers by reducing the need for larger premises, covering for sickness, and improving innovation and retention.

Part-time roles are an ideal way to work when anxiety is an issue. The reduced hours provide sufficient time for decompression. However, many part-time roles offer less meaningful work, but the predictability of the hours may provide stability and structure. They may also enable carers to work when a loved one is at daycare or school.

Zero-hour contracts may at first seem a strange option for autistic people or carers. However, some companies allow you to dynamically say when you are available for work. This may enable some people to work when they are having 'good' days.

'Self-employment' is an option for some people. Think of this as being your own boss. To make this work, you need to have a skill or qualification that others need. It could be working as a private tutor, or an electrician.

Freelance working is project-based self-employment. You are 'employed' for the duration of a project and usually work through a 'contract' agency or directly as a sub-contractor. There are few employment rights, the tax regime is complicated, usually you need specific skills and you have to be very focused.

While self-employment and freelancing may initially appear great, you need to remember that you only get paid for the time worked and, as a result, holidays, sick, caring etc are never covered. You are also outside office politics and the pressure to socialise with colleagues. However, both are precarious and there are none of the protections offered by 'permanent' employment. You must also organise your own pension, do your own taxes, keep books, and constantly search for work. Both options may, however, allow a close alignment between a person's special interests and their work.

Unemployment

Many autistic people are unemployed. Some don't claim Job Seekers Allowance (JSA) or Universal Credit (UC). In 2009, a UK Parliament Early Day Motion, *Don't Write Me Off*, claimed that one-third of autistic adults lack access to benefits or work. Over the intervening years, there have been changes to the system and culture of the DWP, but many people remain suspicious of the DWP and its commitment to helping people with autism. If your loved one hasn't registered as unemployed with the DWP, it is important that they do so to ensure they can survive financially. In addition, they will be able to access the additional support the DWP offers to help them get into meaningful work.

The DWP commissions services with charities and third-party organisations to support people with autism. These services are variable in quality, but some provide meaningful work experience and work hard to build confidence. Sadly, some of these schemes are only available for the under 25s and the over 50s. It is worth asking the job coach about such schemes while being mindful about their suitability.

Some of these schemes are usually described as 'work experience' or as 'back to work' initiatives. Some involve working in shops, stacking shelves, working on allotments, or 'volunteering' in warehouses. Anecdotally, some people have been sanctioned for not attending these schemes. We always ask for the job coach to explain the benefits of such schemes in terms of outcomes. We always ensure that the suggested schemes are suitable for Joe. A job coach has suggested shop-based work experience for Joe despite knowing that he has considerable anxiety around strangers. We gently had to explain that customers are strangers. Another suggested that Joe do work experience with SNAP (a wonderful charity that helps learning-disabled people). Patience and precise explanations will help the job coach find an appropriate scheme.

Local charities and local authorities sometimes have 'job clubs'. Joe has tried a few of these and they are generally very helpful with applications and interview practice. These schemes are generally open to anyone who is vulnerable.

Many people overlook the toll of constantly applying for work and being constantly rejected. People can only take so much rejection, and many become depressed and lose their self-esteem and self-worth. As a carer, this is an area in which you are powerless to make any difference. You can only be there and listen. Being told to stay constantly optimistic is unhelpful, and the notion that 'there's a job out there for everyone' is an absolute lie.

Anecdotally, we have found volunteering and engaging with DWP schemes have helped Joe stay motivated in his search for meaningful work.

Discrimination

When looking for work, either for yourself or your loved one, there is always the worry that any new employer will be unhelpful and unsupportive. For you, there is also the matter of disclosing your other life as a carer, which, as related earlier, can often cause employers to run a mile.

For many autistic people, getting a job is only the beginning of the trauma of work. Some autistic people find a niche in a company and can flourish, but for most, work is difficult. Workplaces have a pecking order, occupied by bullies and cliques that can make the workplace stressful. While a company may have an outwardly inclusive culture, it doesn't mean that such a culture exists internally. A while ago, I asked on social media whether autistic people should disclose. Almost all said no, and many suggested it was the equivalent of painting a target on your back.

This response from @ReluctantTweeter is typical:

> *'I was performing my temp job so well they asked me to train new temps. Interviews came for a perm. position & I tanked the interview b/c "they didn't connect with me on a personal level". I disclosed my autism. When interviews came around again, I was told I was not allowed to apply. They hired the temps I trained. One was hired using the tips I gave him from my interview prep I'd been doing to recover from "not connecting personally" during the other one. Disclosing cost me the opportunity to even interview.'*

Many autistic people report considerable peer and government pressure to work. Many employers have a tick-box attitude to disability accreditations, and some do it simply to satisfy government requirements and initiatives. Some employers sadly don't 'get' autism, and those who do employ autistic people may not accept the need for reasonable adjustments. As discussed earlier, there is plenty of evidence to support the benefit of employing autistic people and there have been several articles in the media talking about the positives of employing autistic people, such increased innovation, focus and dedication to the task at hand.

Discrimination is something that exists and at times cannot be avoided because at the end of the day some people are ignorant. However, there are some steps that can be taken to protect yourself from discrimination and minimise its impact.

When applying for a role check whether the employer is a "Disability Confident employer". If they are there are more likely to be procedures to deal with discrimination. It is also worth joining a union so there is someone who has your back and can provide support when needed.

During the initial agent conversation when applying for new roles I ask the agent three questions:

- What is staff turnover. A high turnover always indicates a probable toxic environment.
- How does the employer feel about carers. I do this to avoid the interview scenario I described earlier.
- Will the employer provide an (indicative) list of interview questions before an interview. A denial of this reasonable request probably is indicative of a less supportive environment.

Many autistic people I have spoken to whilst writing this guide have suggested that disclosing an autism diagnosis can lead to discrimination. However, without disclosing in confidence to HR or senior managers how can you ask for reasonable adjustments or support?

Many autistic people may decide to mask and keep a "low profile" whilst they are at work to avoid the attention of people who are more likely to discriminate against them. However, an alternative approach may be to grow a job that fits your needs.

Some simple ideas that may help:

- Disclosure is your decision. Own who you are.
- Define what success is and means to you. It could be just getting up in the morning.
- Craft a role that plays to your strengths, mindset and relationships.
- Understand your purpose.
- Learn who are allies.

Reasonable adjustments

This is a complicated area and will demonstrate instantly whether a company really understands autism or what an unpaid carer does. Employers have a statutory duty to make reasonable adjustments to ensure disabled workers are not substantially disadvantaged when doing their jobs. Importantly, this duty can involve changing a recruitment process to meet the needs of a candidate.

Over the years, I have watched workplaces change from small rooms hosting a team to large open-plan environments with hot-desking, noise, and bad lighting. Modern office environments may not suit some autistic people.

Some simple 'reasonable' adjustments that would benefit most (even non-autistic) people include:

- Have designated desks for those who need them when they are in the office without enforced hot-desking.
- Have quiet spaces for those who work better in that setting.
- Do not enforce compulsory team building or socialising events.
- Allow for little or zero customer interaction.
- Allow interactions with management to be by messenger or email.
- Allow flexible hybrid working.

When you ask for a reasonable adjustment, please understand, and explain the why and consequence of the need. Many employers may not understand the need and may ask someone to 'assess' your need. They may base their response to any request on that assessment. At times, they may forget who the 'expert by experience' is. It is important to remember that what seems reasonable to you may be viewed as unreasonable by your employer.

The 'Access to work' scheme (HM Government, 2024) may be able to offer some support with equipment, interviews or getting to and from work. The scheme is managed by the DWP. The scheme is designed to enable someone to work, be able to attend work and function effectively in work. The scheme will not pay for reasonable adjustments. For example, I asked my current employer to use "Access to work" to swap my work monitor for a higher resolution monitor to overcome my own physical disability and a reasonable adjustment of having the same desk in a hot desking environment.

Money

Money is quite complicated when you are a carer, but if your finances are methodically organised, the rest may seem less daunting. How you organise your money and that of your loved one is very dependent on your personal circumstances, and will often be guided by what feels right and protects your loved one.

Publicly funded services usually have some form of means testing associated with them, and how the thresholds are applied is variable and sometimes overly complex. Access to services can also be dependent on your family's circumstances and the age of your loved one. It may be necessary to get professional advice to structure your finances and assets to ensure effective support. The whole point is not to avoid charges, but to ensure that whatever wealth your loved one has is not frittered away by unnecessary local authority charges and DWP or other government-department clawbacks. Benefits, or social security as I prefer to call public support for disabled and chronically ill people, has a similar set of complicated criteria and thresholds, product overlaps and hidden clawbacks. It is important to be truthful about your financial position and to inform the authorities of changes in a timely manner.

When organising yours and your loved one's finances and assets, it is worth remembering there are many people who will use every means at their disposal to take everything away from your loved one. Your loved one may be very trusting of others and very naïve about their motives. You may recall the earlier story of the house and the girlfriend…

Social security

'If it exists, claim it' is the only approach to have. The government is quite transparent about the products available and how different thresholds and means testing are applied. Don't rely on general advice from government advisers because many operate in specific product silos. There are many charities, such as the Citizens Advice Bureau, that provide clear advice and may even assist with the complicated forms.

It should be remembered that entitlement to certain products proves entitlement to services without additional paperwork. For example, a PIP confirmation letter trumps a doctor's letter in some circumstances.

The main products that the UK government offers are:

- Carers Allowance
- Carers Credit
- Carers Premium
- Disability Living Allowance
- Personal Independence Payment
- Universal Credit (including ESA and JSA)
- Child allowance
- Attendance Allowance

Please seek advice by talking to other carers, carer organisations and other charities. Understand that the system won't advertise what you may be entitled to and those administering the system are not your friends, but they may be helpful.

Each product has a form. Some forms, like those for PIP and DLA, may seem daunting at first, especially if a submission deadline has been attached. I take a three-stage approach to filling in these forms. I answer each question on scrap paper, I then fill in the form in pencil and after a ponder, I re-ink my words. When thinking about your answers, remember to use adjectives like 'very' and 'extreme'.

On my journey, a request for educational support was rejected by our LA because an eminent clinical psychologist describing Joe as having difficulty with anxiety was considered insufficient proof of his need. This was the psychologist who, as I relayed earlier, sent the LA officer a dictionary with the page holding 'difficulty' highlighted and a new submission with 'difficulty' replaced with 'extreme difficulty'.

The guidance suggests that you describe how your disability affects you. Before you begin please pause, especially if your disability or condition is dynamic. It may be tempting to take an average approach, where you average out how it affects you. I would caution against this because something that may occur with a low frequency may suddenly become far more frequent.

If you decide to take an average approach, how would you measure the impact on you and over what period is appropriate to take an average? For example, I suffer from migraines; some can last 3 to 5 days, but they mostly last a single day. Sometimes I can go a month or more between them, but some months they are one after the other. There are also transitionary effects when I move out of migraine. Taking an average would not present my condition accurately and more importantly may undermine my request.

When you use numbers to quantify the impact of the condition try to avoid precision. For example, if you get disturbed sleep once a week, replace 'once' with 'a few times', because your rollercoaster can very quickly change from once to twice. Similarly if something occurs 4 to 5 times, may be consider using several for similar reasons.

Once aspect that you may overlook is how you have become accustomed to your loved one's condition or behaviour. Think of this as a comparison with the life of a non-carer or that statistical average person. For example, if your loved one talks very loudly, ask yourself whether it could actually be described as shouting. If your loved one pinches or slaps themselves, remember that is self-harm. Say how hard it is, and never gloss over anything.

I always frame this as "Your average is somebody else's nightmare". Fill it in as it is, say it is hard and never use rose-tinted glasses.

You may notice that you end up answering the same question more than once, so be consistent and repeat yourself. If things are hard, say they are hard in *every* answer. Always pull diagnostic paperwork and medical letters into your answers.

Each product has a different burden of proof of need. Usually, a letter of diagnosis is very helpful in providing definitive evidence. I learnt quite early on to scan diagnoses and medical opinion letters for ease of reuse.

Some products have face-to-face assessments to ensure you are not exaggerating, and many people find this part of the process intimidating and intrusive. Again, remember that the assessor is not there to be your friend and understand how they may get paid. Always ask, before agreeing to an assessment, if the assessor is properly qualified and experienced.

Assessments are usually carried out by third parties on behalf of the DWP. These companies employ people with some medical training. For example, you may find your loved one's mental health being assessed by a physiotherapist. That said, the assessor may have had additional training and may have lived experience.

The assessment process is well regulated and knowing these regulations can be extremely helpful. For example, section 1.5.5 of the PIP regulations states '…the types of case that **should not** require a consultation' have exceptions where 'a consultation is likely to be stressful'. The section goes further and specifies that, 'there is strong evidence on which to advise on the case and the consultation is likely to be stressful for the claimant (for example, claimants with autism, cognitive impairment, or learning disability)'. These and similar regulations can be found by entering 'PIP assessment regulations' into Google and picking the links pointing to government websites.

For example, the private company assigned to initially assess Joe for PIP wanted Joe to attend their office in the local Crown Court. The assessment company's letters got more and more threatening and demanding, as they failed to understand the impact that such an assessment would have had on Joe at that time. Moreover, they never provided evidence that the assessor was qualified to talk to Joe. In the end, I forcefully reminded the company of the regulations surrounding autism and anxiety. They finally did a paper-based assessment, but still questioned whether the diagnoses were current, proving my assumptions that they had no idea about autism.

DSA or Disabled Students Allowance provides support for the extra cost of being a disabled student. It may fund a new laptop, or proofreading work, or help with organisation and taxis to and from the uni campus. It does not provide financial support to the student. That said, there is a wrinkle that allows students to claim UC during their course if they have not got a loan. DSA has an assessment process and may require diagnostic proof of conditions and ailments. DSA assessments may include a face-to-face interview. Remember to tell the assessor what is needed.

Carers Allowance (CA) is a product aimed at carers who provide more than 35 hours a week of care. It has terms and conditions. Many complain about the amount of money. There is a clawback linkage between CA and Universal Credit and other products, where the money you receive for CA is clawed back off any other support you receive. It may be worth seeking professional advice before claiming CA to understand whether it is worthwhile and be very mindful of the earnings limits of CA.

If Carers Allowance is not for you, Carer's Credit may be a suitable alternative. Carer's Credit ensures your national insurance is credited while you care (which ensures you get a full state pension).

Carer's Premium is a top-up to existing social security products if you are a qualifying carer.

Child Allowance can be extended beyond 18 if your loved one stays in school for an extra year. If your loved one stays on and you wish to continue to receive the allowance you will need to inform the DWP or the allowance will automatically stop.

When your loved one is no longer in school, you must take them to the Job Centre to sign on. This ensures their national insurance is paid and, more importantly, that they receive some money to live on. You may have to push to see the diversity officer to have a face-to-face talk rather than filling in an online form. Once you are passed the gatekeepers, most DWP staff are friendly and fair. You must *only* talk about your loved one's finances. It is best to ensure there is clear water between your money and theirs. It may be worth thinking about a vulnerable person's trust if your loved one has considerable funds as Universal Credit (UC) and Employment Support Allowance have clawback thresholds.

An interesting component of UC is 'sick pay'. If your loved one is ill, from considerable anxiety, for example, you may be able to ask for a 'Capability for Work' assessment. This comes with a PIP grade mini form and has an associated assessment. It is possible using the regulations mentioned elsewhere to have an advocate (you) complete the form and answer the assessment questions on behalf of your loved one. A doctor's sick note will be required as evidence. This will exempt your loved one from UC seeking work requirements for an extended period.

Many carers act as advocates and appointees for their loved ones. This has legal implications and means DWP officers should only talk to you. However, many forget to read the notes and may call your loved one directly, or refuse to speak to anyone else. (I often wonder how that works for non-verbal and situationally mute people…) When you remind them of your status, some will claim they still need your loved one's permission to talk to you. Just be polite and ask them to read the notes and remind them of the law.

Occasionally, the DWP may decide your claim is 'fraudulent'. This may occur, for example, if you don't inform the DWP of a 'change in circumstance' when you move a significant amount of money from one bank to another. Always be open, but keep the last statement of every closed bank account as you will never know when you will need them. If the DWP does investigate, only answer the questions they ask, and never overshare. Keep transaction notes, so if you have moved money from one bank account to another, make a note of when, why and how much. When the DWP has completed their investigation, they normally write to you, but unless you chase you may not get the 'nothing found' letter.

Many DWP products have sanctions to enforce compliance. Obviously, the sanctions exist to ensure people look for work and attend meetings at their local Job Centre. Applying sanctions to autistic people may be considered discriminatory if the DWP hasn't considered the person's needs. The DWP has a statutory duty to make reasonable adjustments. Sanctions can be avoided if there is a reasonable excuse, but because what is reasonable is not defined by law, there is some discretion in the system. People sometimes forget, and there can be tragic consequences. If you receive a sanction, always appeal, and remind them about autism and any relevant comorbidities.

Trusts

Trusts are used for several reasons, usually for tax planning when gifting assets to loved ones or safeguarding those assets. Trusts provide control and protection over assets. They also have downsides, however, and require management and timely reporting to tax authorities. Moreover, finding appropriate investment accounts to hold money can prove difficult. National Savings and Investments (NS&I) may be helpful.

Control over a trust can be exercised to some degree by the person setting the assets aside, known as a settler. A settler can appoint themselves as a trustee. An outright gift can be spent on anything, because once it is given any control over it is lost, whereas a trust provides a level of protection to ensure the money is spent appropriately.

It is necessary to remember that, once an asset has been surrendered to a trust, it is no longer yours and you can no longer use it as you wish, and you must adhere to the terms of the trust.

In the UK there are several types of trust:

- Discretionary
- Life interest
- Charitable
- Vulnerable person
- Bare

Each of these is intended for a specific purpose and there are compromises to be made with each type. It is essential you are aware of the yearly regulatory and tax burdens, and there may be penalties if a trust is not registered with tax authorities in a timely manner. A trust can be considered to exist when a bank account associated with it is opened.

A discretionary trust usually has a group of beneficiaries. It could simply be all of one's children or grandchildren, for example. Taxes and charges may apply.

A vulnerable person trust is intended for a disabled or vulnerable person. There is a burden of proof required to set one of these up. The trust has tax and charge advantages. Moreover, it is possible to have lifetime exemptions to all charges if certain conditions are met. There are still frequent submissions to be made to the tax authorities.

A bare trust is intended for a single beneficiary who has the right to access the assets held within it at a predefined age. These trusts are often used for children, with the trustee managing the assets until the required age is reached.

Remember, HMRC, while not being able to advise on specific trusts or how you operate them, may be helpful with applying for tax and other exemptions. Registering a trust is a straightforward process using the HMRC online portal. Before registering a trust, you will need to create a Government Gateway ID for the trust. You will be unable to use your own personal identification number. The registration process is done as a wizard, so ensure you have details of who created the trust, date of death, date of birth etc. Similar information is required for each trustee. There is a closing window from the opening of a trust (bank account opening) and registering it with HMRC. Serious penalties may apply if the trust is not registered within the given window.

If a trust is created by a will or a trust deed, you will need copies of these documents to open any linked accounts. Understand that additional money laundering rules may apply.

Power of Attorney

> A few months ago, I had a conversation with an autistic gentleman and his mum about their difficulties with a large organisation. The gentleman is situationally mute, especially when under stress. His mum acts as his advocate and is an appointee at the DWP for that reason. The story illustrates why it may be helpful to consider having Power of Attorney to ensure your loved one's rights are upheld.
>
> The gentleman banks with one of the UK's largest banks. For some unknown reason, the bank locked the man's account meaning he was unable to do any shopping. The gentleman and his mum went to their local branch to get the account unblocked after considerable frustration with their online systems. Despite every effort by mum and appropriate responses from her son, the bank refused to unblock the account. His mum suggested that they accepted head nods and shakes in answer to the bank's questions. Their excuse was that the gentleman was not communicating in an appropriate way. The bank forcefully suggested that his mum returned when she had Power of Attorney (POA).
>
> On my journey, I have been a Power of Attorney for my mum and an appointee (DWP) for Joe. While I can't advise you what is best for you, your loved one or your family, I would hope you think about this because life can get frustrating when you have no authority to act for your loved ones.

The Mental Capacity, Autism and Equality Acts are your friends. Read the statutory guidance and regular updates from learning disability and autism charities.

The Mental Capacity Act says that 'Every adult, whatever their disability, has the right to make their own decisions wherever possible'. There is a duty to provide information in a format that enables them to make an informed choice or decision. The act talks about best interests when a decision is too big for your loved one. Best-interest meetings can be emotive, and without legal authority, your knowledge of your loved one may be ignored, and you can also be excluded. A local authority did this when I was a POA for my mum, but because I only had financial POA I had no say. In their words, 'it was what your mum wished', but knowing my mum and her state of mind at that time (delirium, leading up to the end of her days), I wonder if they had really bothered to ask her and I very much doubt they knew her personality.

At the simplest level, consider being an appointee/advocate when dealing with the DWP and other government and local government departments. The law explicitly (dependent on context) gives your loved one the right to an appointee or advocate. Given my varied experience of people in the DWP, you cannot ensure they will always act in your loved one's best interests. However, if you are accepted as an appointee, you will be expected to attend each meeting with your loved one. On our journey, one DWP officer relaxed this requirement as she knew we were trying to increase our loved one's independence. Others have ignored the appointee-ship and contacted Joe directly. You are the only guarantee that the officers will follow the applicable statutory guidance and respect your loved one's rights

Power of Attorney and deputyship are granted by the Court of Protection and cover financial affairs and welfare (including medical issues). Power of Attorney can be applied for in advance by your loved one. They can ask that is immediately active or only when they are deemed to have lost capacity. To prove a lack of capacity, a medical opinion is required, and patience will be needed while you wait. When you have an opinion, be prepared for a face-to-face chat and robust checks on who you are. You may have to walk through any listed medical conditions, and it may feel as if are repeating yourself as each bank will have a different process.

Deputyships are similar but you will have to apply to the Court of Protection directly or via a solicitor. Expect more robust checks on your motivation and identity, and to verify you loved one's loss or lack of capacity.

Please remember that Powers of Attorney and Guardianship Orders are harder to access when your loved one is non-verbal or is deemed to lack capacity. Expect considerably more hoops to jump through and expenses if your loved one is either. The Court of Protection also needs to confirm that it is in your loved one's best interest.

Discounts

Being a carer can be a financial struggle. You will quickly learn about getting value for money and making pennies go further than ever before. It is worth signing up for discount web sites like those associated with Martin Lewis, 'the money-saving expert'.

Some companies operate discount schemes for carers. The discounts are usually associated with a card that identifies you as a carer. Each scheme generally has an administration charge or fee. Before you part with any money, check that the promised discounts exist, and whether you will make use of them. In my opinion, it is pointless having such a card, since you know you are a carer.

One of the largest bills you will have will be for your council tax. If you are a carer, you may be eligible for a carer's disregard. This is usually a 25% discount, but eligibility is decided by your local council. In addition, you may be eligible for a drop in council tax band if you have modified your home to accommodate your loved one's disability. For example, we have a non-sensory 'sensory' room for Joe. It is expected that the room is used mainly but not solely by your loved one. Again, eligibility is determined by your local authority. If your loved one has a learning disability you may be eligible for the severely mentally impaired (SMI) council tax rebate. An SMI rebate requires medical evidence. The drop in council tax band must be reconfirmed every few years. (A penalty may apply if you don't comply.)

Most water companies operate a discount scheme for people who use more water than expected because of a disability. This scheme is known as 'Watersure'.

Direct payments

Direct payment is the mechanism whereby your local authority outsources its statutory duty of care to you. Each month or week your council will pay you a small sum to find private care and support services for your loved one.

The process is relatively straightforward but is subject to stringent eligibility rules and means testing. Eligibility is determined by a social worker, who will do a mini-PIP assessment of your loved one. Obviously, they may ask to see diagnostic evidence, and they may choose to talk to both you and your loved one. Usually, they ask a series of connected but open-ended questions. A word of caution, never leave them alone with your loved one and always ensure they have appropriate autism training or lived experience. If they have neither, do not let them near your loved one as they may undo months of hard work in building confidence etc.

On our journey, only one social worker 'got it' because she had lived experience, and she was the lady who listened and helped us set up a direct payment with four hours of support a week. The social workers who followed have not really understood and some have made adverse comments or have been accused by our loved one of being stupid for repeatedly asking the same open-ended question. One social worker complained that she had had no appropriate autism training but had been privately reading to improve her knowledge. She was helpful and less confrontational.

After the assessment, the social worker will write a report, but it is up to you to ensure you have a copy. Remember that you have a right to the full report, and it is paramount you check it for inaccuracies and falsehoods. Some may contain inaccuracies, and even blatant lies. The report's contents will form the basis of any offer or entitlement the local authority may make to you. If the authority decides there is insufficient need, ask why and appeal and reapply when you can. Never accept 'no' as an answer.

If your loved one has an entitlement, the finance department of your local authority will focus on your loved one's finances. There are thresholds to determine how much your loved one must contribute. It is essentially a matched funding, so if you don't contribute, they may choose not to. It is worth noting that any checks are on your loved one's finances only. One family with a profoundly autistic loved one I have met on my journey was asked to pay for care and LA support because the family had means. The LA was quite insistent until they were reminded that only their loved one's money mattered. Any assessment should be done in compliance with the 'Care and Support (Charging and Assessment of Resources)' under the Care Act 2014.

Many local authorities operate a card scheme whereby they will issue and control a bank card for you to make electronic payments to your provider. Some may allow payments to a specific joint bank account you control with your loved one. A word of caution, however: the DWP may look at this account and you may have to remind them *forcefully* of its purpose.

We have a specific joint bank account as we control Joe's money rather than the council. However, every quarter we have to submit an expenditure report to our council for them to audit. This can be a chore and our council will always chase us up if we are late with a report.

These council card scheme can reduce the bureaucratic burden on you, but they may not be very flexible and accessing cash to pay for casual things can be difficult. It is horses for courses, at the end of the day.

One of the benefits of a direct payment is choice: you decide who provides the care and support. Most local authorities provide a list of service providers in their local offer. Don't expect any of them to be vetted or appropriate, however, or for the list to be properly maintained. My local authority does vet some. We found a provider that was not initially on our local offer. Before you make a choice, do your own leg work and talk to, even interview, a few. It may seem silly, but it's a good idea to phone them after your chat with additional questions – their responsiveness will tell you a lot. The charity we use was always responsive, but one of the contenders took a whole week to respond.

Always remember that you and your loved one are entitled to advocates.

Inheritance

Some carers and those they care for may inherit money and assets from elderly relatives. For example, my mum left a few bequests to my children and a considerable sum to me. I wanted to pass a significant part of my inheritance to my children to enhance the bequests. The receipt of any inheritance can greatly improve your life but it can also prove to be an unneeded complication. Your loved one may have means-tested support from your local authority and you may be in receipt of social security, both of which have saving and asset thresholds that will instantly apply once any assets are inherited.

It is a relatively straightforward process to avoid these thresholds while still enjoying the benefit of the inheritance by tweaking the will. A will can be changed or varied using a 'Deed of Variation'. Please understand there are applicable hard time limits so you will need to act relatively quickly. The deed can create trusts to hold the money and so protect the inheritance from the state. Obviously, legal advice is required to ensure everything is set up correctly and ensure the inheritance of other parties is not impacted. Trusts are discussed in greater detail elsewhere.

Carer access

Many systems are set up for singular access, that is, a single email address, a single telephone number etc. This can make life difficult when you try to access services on behalf of a loved one. It would sometimes be helpful if multiple email addresses and telephone numbers were supported so notification and confirmation messages can be sent to you as well.

A simple solution is to have a family email address and a cheap pay-as-you-go mobile. Obviously, this is not ideal when you are trying to build confidence and independence, but it can mean that there is a central means of communication that is accessible to both your loved one and all their carers.

Travel and holidays

Travel brings its own set of unique challenges, but with planning and preparation, many can be overcome. Obviously, the type of travel defines the depth of planning and preparation needed. For example, a simple trip to the local shops may not require any planning, but a longer journey in the car may. Other forms of transport each present their own difficulties.

Over the years, we have developed a routine when we travel. The start of the routine begins weeks before with a heads up, followed by little reminders each day as the trip gets closer, and finally 'we are going to...' the day before. On the day, we follow the routine and check everything together to ensure nothing important is left behind, and I am not referring to passports. No matter the journey, we always have a few of our loved one's favourite snacks, some Jelly Babies and Fruit Pastels, a few charging blocks, noise-cancelling headphones, spare cables and some water and fruit juice. We always do a final visual check to ensure everything is packed.

Travelling long distances by car has developed into taking a spare laptop with downloaded cartoons and favourite films. We have found that downloading these to a device is better than relying on a mobile signal and data limits. The car routine also includes story tapes/CDs such as *Harry Potter* or *His Dark Materials* to entertain us all. On longer journeys, we usually stop every two or so hours for everyone to have a break. This avoids the usual 'I need the loo now' issue and provides an opportunity to have a walk etc. Over the years, we have learnt that getting out of the car means everyone has had a better journey. These days we normally stop and pause for half an hour or more in a coffee shop. While this means it can take us longer to get somewhere, no one is fractious or tense.

Flying presents a unique set of challenges, especially if your loved one has never flown before. Many years ago, we discovered 'Special Assistance' by accident, and this is now something we book every time we go on holiday. Special Assistance enables you to pass through any airport with considerably less hassle. It must be booked through your airline rather than directly at the airport, and you need to tell them what you want, whether it is priority boarding, boarding last, seats together etc. However, I always follow up with each airport to ensure they have a record of our needs and, more importantly, to confirm what they think our needs are.

Please understand that some people will see the assistance you and your loved one receive as discriminatory to them. They may argue they have to pay for sitting together, using the VIP lane, and they will have to get up very early to be first to board etc. Ignore them, as they won't be looking at the world from a disabled person's point of view, nor will they be able to see the hoops and proof required for any adjustment to even be considered. Remember, the reasonable adjustments are not to ensure your loved one's equity but to make everyone's journey easier and to comply with the law.

If you use a travel agent online or face to face, you may get told, 'Assistance isn't guaranteed', 'Assistance is only for your loved one',

'Sitting together is only for one carer', 'It is at our discretion', and many similar phrases. Be polite but firm and remind them of the Equality Act (section 6) and the Autism Act. Be precise and persistent in what you ask for. Remind them that you are making everyone else's journey easier.

Many years ago, the Assistance at Heathrow brought a wheelchair for Joe and was quite insistent that it was used. As you'd expect that didn't go down too well with me or Joe. Usually, 'Special Assistance' may give you a lanyard or some paperwork to show that you have assistance. Despite being accompanied during some of your journey through the airport, you can expect toxic comments and non-compliance from some staff.

Some 'Special Assistance' may try to imply that the assistance is only for your loved one and that they will be handled separately to the whole family. Always forcefully resist this nonsense and remind them of the consequences of their insistence. Some airports allow dry runs where you can do a practice run through security etc.

At the boarding gate, always remind the staff that you have 'Special Assistance' and remember to be watchful as some will ignore your request. We have always asked for priority boarding as it suits Joe best and has sometimes been forgotten about. It is a reasonable adjustment and their failure to comply is probably breaking the law. It is worth noting that your priorities trump those of first-class passengers.

Travelling overseas can be far more challenging. It is worth learning a few choice phrases in the local language, especially some about autism. For example, 'Elle tiene autismo' – 'She has autism' – can make a lot of difference when dealing with officials and local police. Just making the effort to briefly explain in a native language can defuse quite a lot of confrontations and clear up a lot of confusion. If you have a few diagnoses or medical letters Google Translate can provide quite reasonable translations for you to take with you. For example, after the pandemic restrictions were removed in the UK, many remained in Spain and exemptions were only available to those with a proven medical exemption. A simple Google translation was sufficient for the local police and hotels in Spain.

When we have travelled to an unfamiliar place, we have used Google Earth to show the area to Joe. This has proved beneficial on several occasions when Joe has asked to see certain landmarks.

The security and whereabouts of your loved ones can be important when in an unfamiliar place. We have found location sharing on mobile phones helpful and others have recently said Apple Airtags and Tile tags are useful for knowing where all your loved ones are.

As technology has moved on, we have periodically upgraded the equipment we take when we travel. Recently we added an Amazon Fire Stick, and this has enabled Joe to enjoy those shows that help when he's feeling overwhelmed. Obviously, the stick is reconfigured before we travel to ensure passwords and so on are up to date. We always ensure we have 'roaming' included when we travel.

Most people take out travel insurance when they go abroad but some may forget to mention autism as a medical condition. We have always declared in order to ensure there is never any issue with a claim. I recall one insurance company wanting an additional £100 to cover Joe. When I asked why, they said it was in case there was a 'psychiatric-based claim' (obviously they knew a lot about autism…).

Many people struggle to go on any form of holiday, let alone abroad. When Joe was little, we used to take his bedding, cuddly toys, and his baby blanket. While we can't say whether it is familiarity or simply the detergent smell or the smell of home, it has helped and enabled us to travel further than the UK. Speaking to other carers, some teenagers still take their cuddly toys with them. Occasionally stuff can be overwhelming, especially more so when not at home. For these occasions, we used to pack small Lego kits or new toys. Lego has always proved to be a great distraction and has helped restore calm, and I am a great believer in Lego therapy.

On this journey, we have found hotels are better than bed and breakfasts. It may sound strange, but we always return to the same hotel in Mallorca where we always have a wonderful holiday. This hotel understands Joe, and it feels like a home from home. The staff are the same year in, year out, and that makes a huge difference.

Local authorities

Your journey will be at times dominated by your relationship with your local authority. Your relationship will probably begin when you first apply for support in school. Many SEN parents and unpaid carers have very strong opinions about their local authorities, and some describe the relationship as toxic. I have baggage with my local authority and at times it can colour my judgement.

Burrows *et al* (2021) were commissioned by the NHS to report the impact of COVID-19 and the future of caring. Their report stated, in the context of statutory services, that 'Local authority assessment and support was almost universally perceived as inadequate. Incomplete and sometimes actively distressingly in its delivery.' Binky Brewer describes her LA as, 'Worse than useless. And they care even less...'

Many carers describe the relationship in terms of the battles they have had to fight. Julie Jones succinctly explains this aspect as, 'The LA? No. Nothing good never came from them without their hand being forced.'

Cullen *et al* (2019) examined the drivers of complaints and disagreements in England's SEN system. They reported that 'in 19 cases where the LA had initially refused to assess the child's need, but then agreed to do so after mediation or a tribunal order, all the children proved to have complex needs'. They concluded that 'the underpinning principles of the Warnock Report remain relevant: the human right to education, accurate assessment of needs, and professionals working in partnership with parents. When these are in place in practice, our data indicate that SEN disagreements will be prevented or more easily resolved.'

Before you start panicking, pause, and consider the three drivers that underpin the systems we have: budget, policy, and the law. Understand how and why policy is framed, why budgets are set and the role of the law. Ideally, the law should underpin all policy, but the law is not mathematically precise, and is filled with imprecise and fuzzy concepts like 'reasonable', 'needs', and 'disability'. Policy is also shaped by the culture of society and different organisations, and both create the procedures that the organisation operates by. Unlike the law, budgets are precise and constrained by the government. Because these procedures are also budget-focused, they contain thresholds to 'assess' needs and disability. Most of the people who apply these procedures are not experts and rely on internal experts and professional reports to inform their decisions. These people are sometimes placed under enormous political pressure to preserve their budgets.

Statutory duties

Local authorities have many statutory duties, which are things they must do by law. They include social care, public health, child protection and education. These duties are scattered across various Acts of Parliament and described clearly in the statutory guidance that accompanies each.

Acts that are relevant to autism include the Autism Act (2009), Children and Families Act (2014), Health and Care Act (2022), Disability Discrimination Act (1995), Equality Act (2010), Mental Health Act (1983), and Care Act (2014). There are also codes of practice and strategies that clarify duties and expectations. These include the SEN code of practice, autism strategies and NHS Long Term Plans.

Recently, the UK Parliament published an overview of autism policy and strategy (Garrett *et al*, 2023). While the report describes how far there still is to go, it provides a critical overview of duties and expectations. It also lists the Acts and strategies that underpin those expectations.

You may be wondering why this matters: in answer, it is a striking statistic is that 96% of SEN tribunals rule in favour of parents (2022-23). Consider also what happened when we applied for an 'assessment of need' from adult services – we were told there was an 18-month waiting list. I wrote to the responsible cabinet member and asked for a meeting. At the meeting, I reminded the councillor and a senior officer what the law and the council's own website stated. We had our assessment in weeks.

You may wonder why it appears many LAs do this, and the simple answer is that it comes down to their perception of need, and their finite budgets and resources. Every authority will allocate a finite budget to specialised services, like SEN support, and will exercise some form of triage before allocating some of the budget to your loved one. Similarly, there will also be a finite number of specialised SEN school places.

Please understand that the management of their budget and resources is their problem. Use the law, hold them to timescales and always remember a statutory duty means MUST.

Organisational structure

Most local authorities are organised by competencies. For example, there will be a department for adult social care and another for education. Some of these departments may have overlapping competencies, especially when transitions are involved.

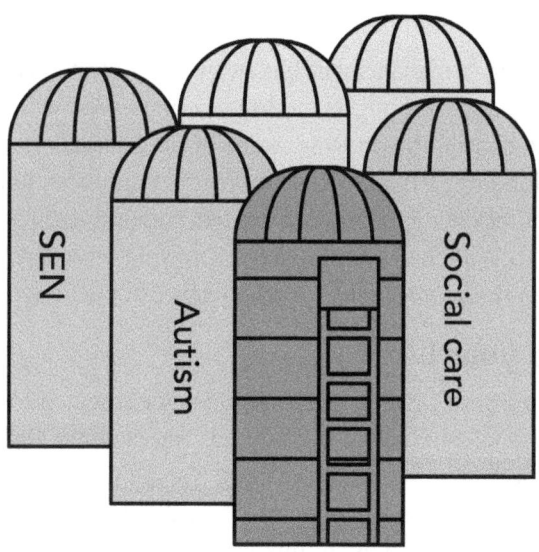

Some departments may have a 'silo mindset' and appear to rarely talk to each other. This silo-based thinking may also be enforced by incompatible IT systems. Some LAs have tried to resolve this by creating 'super silos', by grouping together linked competencies like child and adult services. Some authorities also merge departments periodically to improve efficiency, but there are consequences of reorganisation and of having larger departments, for example there is a risk of a dilution of experience and some managers are bureaucrats with little affinity for the merged services they have been put in charge of. That said, with larger departments you may benefit from faster responses, and if the 'team' knows the competencies of each member, they can be more effective. If the managers have lived experience, you will have far better outcomes and less frustration.

As an example of the dilution of expertise, my LA had a specific autism team several years ago but it was merged into the learning disability service, then mental health (illness not well-being) services, and most recently into a generic adult service. Initially, we always had the same autism-trained social worker. In recent years, however, we get whoever is assigned, and generally they appear to have no knowledge of autism.

As a carer, a silo-based operation means I must constantly repeat the same story and I must fight the same tired old battles constantly. A super silo means I may only have to tell the story once, but finding the right person is another matter.

Your local authority's management has two parts – elected councillors, who make policy and set budgets, and senior managers, who implement the policies and control the budgets. Some of the councillors will have responsibility for a department like a government minister, and others run scrutiny committees like parliamentary select committees. The managers are equivalent to Whitehall civil servants. Knowing who is who is important when things go wrong, or when you can't get a straight answer.

Contacting your LA

Before contacting your LA, it is worth doing some research to avoid the frustration of the telephone merry-go-round. For example, I recently wanted to speak to someone about making a small change to how we spend some of Joe's direct payment. Logically, I phoned the direct payment team who directed me to financial services, who directed me to Adult Social Services, who directed me to the social work team.

Most LAs have a Competence Management Information System (CMIS) listing most managers and their competences. It may be quicker to directly email a manager with your query than spend hours on the phone being transferred between answering machines. Expect an underling to contact you rather than the manager.

It is worth remembering that LAs are not always the most responsive of organisations. It is also worth remembering that the person you contact may not deal with your enquiry or question. Depending on their position in the organisation, policies surrounding decision making and basic workflow, someone else may respond to you. Moreover, your request may even involve a 'panel', where managers and experts make collective decisions. It is always worth constantly following up to ensure they respond to you. Always remember that panels are committees, and as such they will always have minutes.

Accessing services

Local authorities offer many services, but many require proof of need. For example, when we first contacted child services, we were told our loved one was not 'disabled enough'. Whether that was an officer having a bad day or a poor attempt at gatekeeping I shall never know. Many triages are best described as mini-PIP assessments. Some of these assessments will be frequently repeated to 'confirm' need. Most are done by social workers or a clinical or educational psychologist. You may be expected to provide access to medical records or provide some medical proof of need. If you are trying to access services on behalf of an adult, expect some GDPR nonsense. Please note that not all officers will be 'official' and some will happily engage with you.

On occasion, you may transition between services because of age thresholds. This is like the transition from DLA to PIP. Please understand that not all transitions run smoothly due to different assessment thresholds and permissions. For example, for Joe to successfully transition from child to adult services, he was asked for his permission for the LA to share his data with itself. Similarly, Joe had to give his permission for us to act on his behalf. I wonder how that works, with non-verbal, situationally mute people and those with no capacity?

If your loved one has an assessed need, the authority will do a financial triage assessment to determine who pays. This is why you need to protect your loved one's assets and savings.

There are two service options: direct services organised by the authority, and those organised by you and paid for via direct payments. The services offered in your authority's area are normally listed in their 'local offer' of 'approved' service providers. Some of the approved providers may be inappropriate for your loved one and you may find better alternatives yourself.

Carers assessment and reviews

Your local authority will carry out carer assessments on request. The assessments are normally carried out by social workers, but you may have to wait a while. Hopefully, you will get a social worker with some experience of autism, but don't hold your breath because they can be rarer than Dodo eggs. That said, many are empathetic and will listen if you guide them.

If your loved one is registered with the LA, they may also carry out an infrequent review to assess their needs and hence determine whether they can continue to access services. Both may be done at the same time.

The social worker will probably ask you and your loved one lots of open, circular, and deficit-based questions. The process can be emotional and draining as you tell the same story over and over, and answer the same questions you have answered on many previous occasions. The social worker will write a few reports; remember to ask for copies, and once you receive your copies you will see in black and white how different your life is to most people's.

You may ask what the assessment will do for you and what difference it will make; I have never had an answer I can grasp. However, for me, it is always a reflective exercise to see how far we have come and how far we still must go. In my mind's eye, I see an egg timer running down, and the assessments help me plan my next steps.

Homelessness

Homelessness is a complex issue and includes people sleeping rough, using hostels, 'sofa surfing' etc. Autistic people make up a significant proportion of the homeless population. In one town, nearly 75% of rough sleepers were autistic (Garratt & Flaherty, 2021). An earlier study by Churchard *et al* (2019) stated, 'This study has provided initial evidence that autistic traits are over-represented among homeless people; and that autistic homeless people may show a distinct pattern of characteristics and needs'.

Many are at increased risk of homelessness because of a lifetime of social and economic disadvantage, including low educational attainment (caused by a lack of support), difficulties in finding and keeping jobs, and social exclusion. Once homeless, support services become even more inaccessible. It is important to remember that autistic people also have a heightened risk of mental illness, which substantially increases the risk of homelessness.

In the UK, accommodation offered to homeless single people under 35 is limited to a space in a shared house or hostel. Both are likely to aggravate social anxiety and sensory processing difficulties.

Some local authorities may offer supported living, but supported living varies and may be include a room in a shared house or a self-contained flat with some on-site support. If your loved one lives at home, accessing supportive living or social housing may prove difficult, without making them intentionally homeless. We have spoken to Joe about his feelings if we made him intentionally homeless so he could have his own home, he said he would feel 'abandoned'.

Many autistic people live in their family home into middle age, and they may be reliant on their family for financial support. In the event of a relationship breakdown, such as the death of a parent, a serious disagreement, MHA sectioning or the development of a serious mental illness, they may be forced out of the family home. Autistic people who have been sectioned are at increased risk of homelessness if there is no one to support them upon release.

Local authorities have a duty to assess and house people who are not intentionally homeless and have a 'priority need' when they make an application. However, autistic people may not meet the priority need criteria and they must demonstrate that they are vulnerable for a 'special reason'. Not every autistic person will have the energy to deal with the local authority and petition that they are vulnerable.

Repeat homelessness can be particularly problematic. Simon explains: 'I would be devastated to be homeless again. I would worry about being out in unsuitable shared accommodation particularly around noise and cleanliness.'

What can you do to protect your loved one from being homeless? There is no easy answer, but you could:

- Let them live at home. I understand this may be difficult for many due to personal circumstances.
- Ensure your loved one knows their rights.
- Ensure timely access to mental health support.
- Leave assets in a trust for your loved one.
- Buy a small flat or house for your loved one (in trust).

Chapter 4:
Building understanding

Before I began this journey, I don't even recall being aware of the word 'autism', let alone knowing what it meant. Obviously, when Joe entered my life, all that changed. My knowledge was based on my lived experience and I became an overnight 'expert' (with hindsight, only based on my perception of Joe). Over the years, Joe (and others) have taught me that autism is complicated. At times it has more moving parts than a space shuttle, but unlike the shuttle there is no Haynes manual.

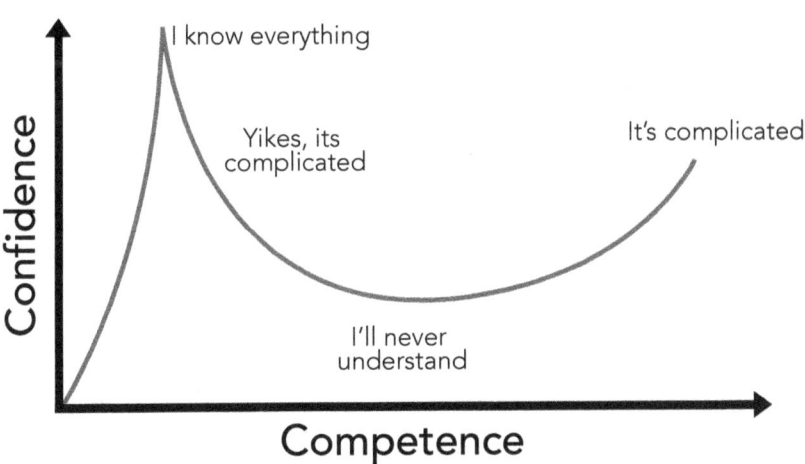

This section is about building your knowledge and understanding to increase your resilience and informed responsiveness. It also provides information about a range of reading materials that may increase your understanding and acceptance. It also gives information about the power of words, and how to spot therapies that are snake oil.

Reading and listening

My home and Kindle are filled with books and journals based on my passions; engineering, history and autism. Books and journals have provided a solid foundation that has enabled me to support Joe effectively. Blogs, podcasts and websites – especially those created and maintained by autistic people – have kept my knowledge current with autistic thinking.

Personally, I avoid any media that I classify as 'self-help' or that advise you how to 'cure' your loved one. I also avoid media focused on ABA and PBS therapies. This is based on my scepticism surrounding these approaches.

Books and journals

There are many technical 'autism' books explaining genetics and theories, and many of these are impenetrable or use too many big words. I generally avoid books by famous scientists and clinicians who have been less than sympathetic to autistic people, especially when their current work is controversial and considered harmful by autistic people. I will, however, read their peer-reviewed research papers.

Some of autism journals have free email subscriptions that notify you of new peer-reviewed papers. Many such papers are initially open access, but if not, many authors will send you a free pre-print copy if you email them asking nicely. I subscribe to *Autism*, *Journal of Autism and Developmental Disorders*, *BMJ* and *Autism Research*.

One of my favourite technical books is *Autism*, by Sue Fletcher-Watson and Francesca Happe (Routledge, 2019). It clearly and concisely explains autism without the big words, and it is written in a style that is relaxed and very readable. Others I'd recommend are those by Dr Luke Beardon.

The following non-technical books are among my favourites and the ones I normally buy and send to relatives when they get to the point of wishing to know more. The first book that put everything into perspective for me was *NeuroTribes* by Steve Silberman (Allen & Unwin, 2015). For me, this book is worth a Nobel Prize just for the number of people it has helped. *Life, Animated* by Ron Suskind (Kingswell, 2016) clarifies the value of naming what Joe is dealing with so I can deal with it directly. It helped me to understand that I will always be needed to support Joe.

There are several books that explain autism from an autistic person's point of view. Of these, I recommend *The Reason I Jump* (Sceptre, 2015) and *Fall Down 7 Times Get Up 8* (Sceptre, 2018) by Naoki Higashida, a non-verbal autistic person from Japan. These books explained so much to Joe's late Nan. *Untypical* (Mudlark, 2024) and *What I Want to talk about* (Jessica Kingsley, 2022) by Pete Wharmby are also helpful. A few people will point out that a book by an autistic person is only one person's view of autism, but the simple answer to that is to read many, I say.

Many carers have recommended the following books to me:

- *Abilities in Me* by Gemma Kier (Independent, 2019). This is aimed at a younger audience.
- *The Girl With Curly Hair* by Alis Rowe (Lonely Mind Books, 2013).
- *Communication Alternatives in Autism* by Edlyn Pena (McFarland, 2019) is aimed at carers of non-verbal people.

Social media and websites

The large autism charities in the UK, like the NAS, Autistica, and 'Ambitious about Autism', have large and informative websites. Your local council's website will host their 'local offer' listing many local services and support. If you can't find what you want on these sites, Google is your friend. When using Google please be precise in what you ask for.

'Autability' has lots of helpful information: www.autability.co.uk. Chris Bonnello's site 'Autistic not weird' also has lots of brilliant information and can be found at https://autisticnotweird.com.

A few autism sites have free email subscriptions. 'Spectrum News' is one I regularly use and can be accessed at www.spectrumnews.org. Some of the news is focused on research but occasionally there is a golden nugget of information. It is useful if you want to understand current thinking and legislative changes. The site also has a useful 'Autism 101' section that explains many issues in a clear manner.

'Autism Eye' is a UK-based autism website for parents and carers. There are many articles that carers may find useful. They also frequently publish a magazine that is available through an email subscription. I have learnt a considerable amount from the magazine.

'Autism Europe' is a pan-European organisation funded by the EU. It has an email subscription service to keep you informed of all things related to autism. Their website is at www.autismeurope.org/ and contains many useful reports. My favourite report explains autism's contribution to human progress.

I follow many autistic people and unpaid carers on X (formerly known as Twitter). Quite a few peer-reviewed papers are also announced on X. If you decide to use X, remember the rules about using interactive social media.

X also has 'Spaces', an interactive form of podcast. I have found the space 'Sharing the load as an unpaid carer', organised by Marie Martin (@martinimarie), helpful in dealing with issues from a carer's point of view.

Video may be a little more accessible for some people so the following is a short selection of videos from YouTube that explain various aspects of autism. Please be aware that some of the themes may be triggering:

- Culture and how it defines autism from an anthropological perspective by Richard Grinker, 'Culture and Autism, Anthropological Perspectives', available at https://youtu.be/vKMXS5Y8e7I (accessed May 2024).
- Cultural perspectives of autism by Richard Grinker, 'Invention/Reinvention of Autism', available at: https://youtu.be/x1fsQT9M354 (accessed May 2024).
- Neurodiversity – the key that unlocked my world by Elisabeth Wiklander, 'Neurodiversity key', available at: https://youtu.be/Qvvrme5WIwA (accessed May 2024).
- The beautiful reality of autism by Guy Shahar, 'Autism reality', available at https://youtu.be/S8Nb2FDmQo4 (accessed May 2024).
- Why everything you know about autism is wrong by Jac den Houting, 'AUTISM what you know', available at https://youtu.be/A1AUdaH-EPM (accessed May 2024).

Blogs and podcasts

There are many blogs that explain caring and autism very well. My go-to blog on autism is Ann Memmott's which is available at http://annsautism.blogspot.com. This blog has a huge amount of well-written information on autism from an autistic person's perspective.

Another excellent favourite of mine is 'Thinking person's guide to autism', https://thinkingautismguide.com. This has up-to-date thinking and the points are always well made and explained clearly.

I have found the weekly podcast by 'Autism Science Foundation' – https://asfpodcast.org –very useful in explaining the complexities of autism without the big words. They are not afraid to explore some of the more controversial areas of autism and regularly interview researchers.

Helen Jeffries, or the 'Autistic Civil Servant', writes a thoughtful blog that explores what it is like to be autistic. It is a mixture of philosophy, current affairs and just autism. It helps me think about things from a different perspective.

Words matter

The language of autism is filled with jargon and words with unintended and contextually based consequences. Several words are deeply offensive, and others may have fatal consequences because of the anxiety that is usually bundled with autism. Some people will interpret this as 'woke', or as a restriction on their freedom of speech. It is neither, it is simply about reducing the toxicity that is very harmful to our loved ones.

Ask yourself how you would respond if someone called you a 'retard' or criticised your work to distract people from their own failings? Most of our loved ones fiercely believe in social justice and many wear their hearts on their sleeves, and the impression and unfairness in your words can quickly escalate situations. Always pause and momentarily reflect on the consequences of your verbal and written words. And always remember it is better to be a fireman than an arsonist.

There are times when you will need to speak for your loved one. Speak with and for your loved one. Try not to speak over your loved one and be mindful of your loved one's opinions, but remember there may be times when your loved one is situationally mute.

Always be prepared to defend your loved one. Over the years, we have learnt how and when to help. Once, during a visit to the DWP, an aggressive gatekeeper demanded to know why Joe had dared to enter the Job Centre. Targeted aggression can make Joe selectively mute, and it is a clear sign that intervention is required. I recall asking the gentleman if he would kindly wind his neck in and have some patience. When he backed down and calmness was restored, Joe told him that he had an appointment.

Labels

Why do labels matter, you may ask? Think about your own perception of others and how you describe, or *label,* them. Some labels are *sticky* and attach themselves to people and follow them around like millstones or badges of honour. For many, the label *becomes* them. If a person is called 'stupid' their whole life, or 'naughty', is it any wonder that they might begin to believe it?

Children spend considerable time with teachers and adults who use labels. There is a perception, for example, that autistic and ADHD children are 'naughty', and this can be reinforced by adults who describe and label children as such who don't always conform or follow instructions to the letter. Consequently, other children might ostracise autistic and ADHD children in order to avoid being seen as naughty by association. This is probably reinforced by the ignorant bias of other parents and parental gossip at the school gates, and teacher's gossip in the staff room. A sad consequence of this is that autistic or ADHD children are often blamed over others, or not believed, because they are perceived as naughty. In the context of bullying, this often arises when an autistic person verbally or physically lashes out at a bully who has tormented them and the bully is believed but the victim isn't. Please remember, bullies can also include teachers.

'Naughty' is one of those very sticky labels, and it can impact lives. If you are interested, look up Prof Amanda Kirkby's work on the make up of the UK prison population.

Other sticky labels include 'overdramatic', 'weird', 'sensitive', 'emotional', 'lazy', 'quirky' and 'rude'. As you are aware, autistic people may have meltdowns, which some people class as tantrums. Some people describe autistic people as overdramatic, divas, over-sensitive or over-emotional because of these incidents. The long-term consequences of persistently labelling your loved one with these traits is masking. Long-term masking is clinically dangerous and can increase the risk of serious mental health issues (Sedgewick *et al*, 2021).

Insults

A recent *Forbes* article (Purlang, 2021) describes why you should not use insults based on disability. Historically, people have used words once used by doctors to describe people with intellectual and/or developmental disabilities. While these were acceptable many years ago, they now carry a huge social stigma, especially for people with visible and invisible disabilities. Words like 'retard', 'moron' and 'idiot' are considered by many to be offensive. 'Retard' is considered by many disabled people to be equivalent to the 'N' word.

In recent times, as the number of autistic people has increased many people have started using 'autism' and 'autistic' to insult other people. These insults are based on historical stereotypes which really don't reflect the current thinking about autism.

For example, some politicians have described other politicians as 'autistic' when they are resistant to change or are not very eloquent when they make speeches. Several years ago, an opposition politician described Prime Minister Gordon Brown as 'faintly autistic'. Many countries have similar examples.

At the end of 2022, Greta Thunberg, an autistic climate-change activist, was trolled by a gentleman with a large car collection. Greta responded to the message by suggesting that his car collection was inversely proportional to the size of his penis. Greta's tweet went viral. The gentleman posted a video further mocking Greta.

A journalist responded to Greta's tweet in support of the gentleman. The journalist used 'autistic' to describe Greta which, from my point of view and many in the autistic community, was used to undermine her. The journalist later revised the tweet, removing 'autistic' following community wide outrage. The journalist cited Greta Thunberg's own social media profile as her reason for including the fact that Greta Thunberg is autistic in her response.

It is important to remember that labelling someone as autistic in relation to a point they are making about something unrelated to autism is unnecessary and can be hurtful and undermining.

Person first

This refers to how a disabled person chooses to be described. Many people, especially 'professional' people prefer 'person with a disability' rather than 'disabled person'. The person first or 'with' approach says the person is a person who happens to have a disability. The other approach assumes that the disability is an important part of the person's identity.

As autism is genetic in origin, it is an integral part of an autistic person and most autistic people prefer 'autistic' over 'with autism'. However, this is not a hard and fast rule, and it is best to ask about preference.

Using 'with autism' can prove very controversial on social media. Many eminent scientists and celebrities have been 'flamed' for using 'with'. So, think about the context and consequences.

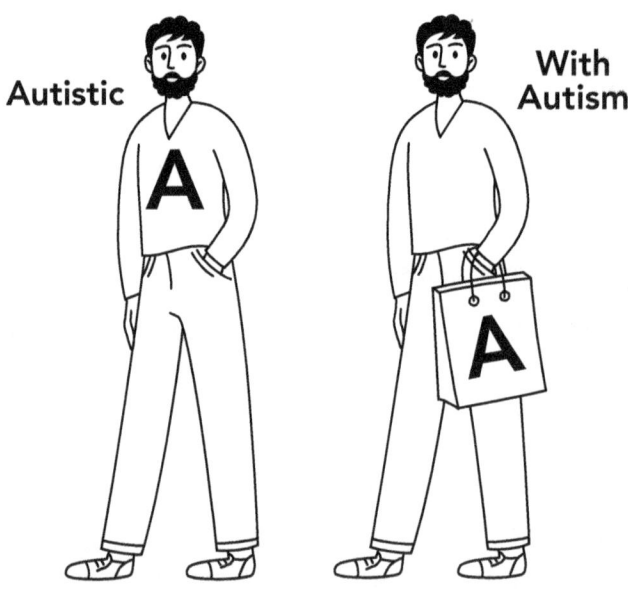

A similar argument can be made to use 'autism' instead of 'autism spectrum disorder' (ASD). Some will say this is because the latter is too medical, and others will say it is because it is based on the social model of disability. Joe explains it this way:

> *'Autism is the ability to drive, and ASD is the license society demands you have'.*

Unintended phrases

Any language is filled with colloquial speech and euphemisms. Some of these can be controversial and some may be deeply offensive. Like the 'with autism' described above, many of these will depend on context and who you are in conversation with. Some are best avoided altogether. It is best to avoid well-meaning euphemisms like 'special needs' and 'differently-abled' because they are overused and are rarely used by autistic people.

'You don't look autistic' is usually intended as a compliment but only demonstrates how ignorant you are. Autistic people look the same as everyone else. They come in all shapes and sizes, and if there was a particular look, I would hope *Vogue* would have picked up on it by now.

'We are all a little autistic' or 'faintly autistic' demonstrates that the person has assumed that autism on a linear scale, with non-autistic folk around 0% to 10%, Asperger Syndrome at 40 to 50% and profound or severe autism at 100%. Autism is binary, you are either autistic or you are not.

I imagine autism to be a surface that dynamically changes with mood and environment. The surface is shaped into hills, valleys, and sinks. The sinks represent meltdowns and shutdowns and the hills and valleys comorbidities or the other conditions that are bundled with autism.

Perception of autism

| Normal People | Aspergers | Classic Autism | Severe Autism |

0% ————————————— Autism ————————————— 100%

Some people believe it is possible to overcome autism, usually described as 'autism moms'. Many autistic people will point out that autism can never be overcome as it's part of who they are.

Some people believe autism and ADHD are 'fashionable', and that they somehow get you special concessions at work and in education. At first glance, their claims may seem credible given that the prevalence of autism is increasing, but even a shallow dive can quickly unravel their claims. Following the COVID pandemic, there was a trend on TikTok of people claiming to be autistic to get special treatment. The reality is obviously quite different. Claiming that autism is fashionable undermines decades of advocacy and makes autism seem almost trivial.

Managing anxiety

Most people have very limited experience of real anxiety and may think that it is the 'butterflies' they experience when they do something new or go to an interview, rather than the deadly thing it can be. They forget that anxiety can impact someone's self-esteem.

If anyone is suffering badly from anxiety, it is best to avoid critical phrases like 'stop being a diva', 'it's not that loud', 'stop being a baby' etc, as they will only make the anxiety circular and will guarantee a meltdown or shutdown.

Many autistic people have heightened anxiety. Some may also have a diagnosis of an anxiety disorder. Heightened anxiety can be very problematic and without management or strategies to deal with it, it can lead to a loss of sleep and to self-harm. In extreme circumstances it can result in suicide ideation.

This is one of the more complex areas of supporting an autistic person. An environment, the number of people, the current mood, an event or what was recently said can seriously affect someone's anxiety. The situation can be dynamic and requires some knowledge of the autistic person. Some words or sounds can be triggering, some are more context-specific. Ideally, it is best to speak with the person and be mindful and positively reactive.

Aspergers

Dr Hans Asperger is a controversial figure. His name was associated with type 1 autism (DSM-5) in the early 1980s as Asperger Syndrome. Because of his Nazi associations, many feel this term shouldn't be used. However, it is complicated, because many people have been diagnosed with Asperger Syndrome and many of these people proudly identify as 'Aspies'. Some people are intolerant of this because of the association with Dr Asperger. In short, using the term 'Aspergers' needs to be approached with caution.

Functioning

Autism is split into categories that are supposed to reflect the level of their support needs and how well a person functions. This need is expressed in phrases like 'high functioning', and 'low functioning', and with words like mild, severe and profound.

Functioning, as a term and a concept – that is, high or low functioning – are controversial. It is sort of based on apparent or 'visible' cognitive ability and communication skills. A non-verbal autistic person may be thought of as low functioning. The tests used to determine 'functioning' are based on non-autistic people, and as such may underestimate the ability of an autistic person. Moreover, an autistic person may function more effectively when they use a device to communicate. An example of this is the online autistic community where many non-verbal people can be highly articulate as their typing speaks for them. Please remember, *The Reason I Jump* book was written by a non-verbal gentleman.

Some people say that 'high-functioning autism' is the only type accepted by society but it's important to consider whether that is simply because it is more invisible due to the autistic person masking.

Some people believe that 'high-functioning' people take resources away from 'low-functioning' people, despite their needs being profoundly different. In a way, labels cause this conflict.

Controversially for some, I think we need better descriptive words because the current pushback against functioning labels doesn't help those who are not rocket scientists or who are very disabled. *The Lancet* recently discussed the controversy surrounding the use of 'profound' to describe autism (Lord, 2021).

Please remember that the current labels also tend to ignore those in the middle who also struggle.

Never-use terms and phrases

On this journey you will encounter people who will see you and your loved one as a burden. You already know about the once-medicalised words used to insult and cause offence, such as 'retard', and you will hear them, but some words and phrases will sometimes be very cutting or triggering. Many are based on ignorance and some on sheer hate.

'Autism is a disease' is a good example. This phrase is totally ignorant and is based on the falsely claimed epidemic narrative. It makes autism sound like leprosy, something unclean and to be avoided.

Vaccinated were they	We're all a little autistic	Autism is a disease
They need a good slap	Having a tantrum	Autism is made up
Faintly autistic	Only boys get autism	Severe end of the spectrum
None when I was a child	Recover from autism	Mild end of the spectrum
Faking – they make eye contact	Caught it off Tik-Tok	Too much screen time
They're not disabled	We all get anxious	Bad parenting

'Vaccinated were they?' is often a sign of someone trying to be clever. Again, totally ignorant and caused by a single discredited doctor and numerous unscrupulous journalists.

'They just need a good slap' shows a total failure to understand people having a bad day. Sometimes a meltdown can appear as a tantrum, but resorting to violence will only make matters worse.

This way of seeing autism is sometimes underpinned by medical professionals who don't understand what autism is. For example, a mum took her young daughter to A&E following an overdose. The mental health nurse told the mum that 'it was part of autism'. Think about the consequences of that simple phrase.

Kindness

While it may seem obvious, kindness is your greatest helper. You can be kind and still be critical. You may know the phrase 'equal and opposite reaction' from science, but you may forget that this is just as important as words. Words can diffuse or chastise, praise or cause sorrow. It simply means if you push, expect a push back.

Consider how you respond when you learn someone's grandmother has died. You probably say something like, 'I'm sorry for your loss' because you know it's not about you but the person who is in pain. It is the pain you seek to diminish with your words.

Kindness is also helpful in defusing situations. It clearly demonstrates that you are not judging or criticising someone and that you are prepared to listen. It is always worth remembering how little you know about a person.

Puzzle piece

Autism has been represented by a puzzle piece for many years, but for a growing number of people its use is controversial. Many charities and autism-focused businesses have used or still use a puzzle piece in their logos. Many people have puzzle piece lanyards and badges in the shape of a puzzle-piece ribbon.

The puzzle piece suggests that something is missing and reinforces the deficit-focus many people associate with autism. A blue puzzle piece is problematic for many autistic people as it represents the logo of a large American charity with controversial views.

Many autistic people prefer a multi-coloured infinity ellipse as it signifies a spectrum of infinite difference and possibilities.

Therapies

Autism is filled with controversial therapies. Some are damaging to health, some are rip-offs, and others carry long-term mental health consequences. Understanding which therapy is appropriate is important for your financial security, and for the health of your loved one.

Autism therapy is big business and there are many things claimed to be therapeutic and suitable for autistic people. Some people will even claim to be able to cure autism.

On my journey, my scepticism has increased, and I would caution and advise you:

- Never to be taken in by glossy brochures or sales pitches.
- Always do your own research using reputable sources.

- Ask for the contact details of people providing testimonials.
- Check the scientific literature – Google Scholar is a great source.
- Always ask actual autistic people for their opinions.
- Always ask actual parents/carers for their opinions.
- Always ask if they are regulated.
- Always ask if they are licensed.
- Always ask about their relevant qualifications.
- Always ask about their lived experience.
- Remember that you know your loved one better than any therapist.

All therapies and treatments have consequences, so be sure your choice is right for your loved one. Some therapies are potentially dangerous with hidden long-term consequences. Always be sceptical and ask if you can speak to other parents/carers before parting with money. The UK-based 'Thinking About Autism' organisation has a large list of many therapies. Their website may be a good starting point if you wish to go down a formal therapy route. Please understand that many autistic people have valid opinions about therapy and it is worth asking them about the consequences of any therapy you are considering. Brause (2024), writing in *Psychology Today*, discusses the harm that inappropriate therapy can do. Always do your own *independent* research.

How to access therapy

Access to therapy depends on your loved one's age and needs. Some therapy is also dependent on your ability to pay. On my journey, I have learnt that many services are not geared to the needs of autistic people. Many therapeutic services have a triage gate you and your loved one need to get through. Some will use the triage gate to exclude by blaming everything on autism. In reality, they are using autism as an excuse to hide their lack of services because they have commissioned none. Others may use the excuse to hide their waiting lists or their own ignorance.

The most difficult part of therapy is knowing what will work, what is appropriate, and whether can it be accessed. This comes down to effective signposting. When I started on this journey, I had no idea where to go. I recall meetings with council officers and other professionals who made sympathetic noises but offered little direction.

A 'modern' health system works by contract, i.e. someone commissions a service from a provider and the contract will describe what is to be provided. Autism and ADHD are sometimes overlooked. So how do you overcome a lack of services or exclusion when it is blamed on autism? There is no guaranteed approach, sadly, but understanding the laws on discrimination, autism and equality, and continually badgering, does appear to work. The guides that accompany each act frame the law and usually provide helpful examples. The ECHR and UNCHRDP are also useful and they clearly spell out the rights of your loved one.

Sometimes, approaching a manager directly, bypassing the gatekeeper, can provide the outcome you need. Networking with other carers and professionals can also help, as they may be able to directly signpost you to bypass the gatekeeper, which can save you months of anguish and frustration.

Several years ago, Joe needed professional support and we were increasingly out of our depth. In the past, we had great support from CAHMS and during a telephone triage we were told the issues were caused by autism. At this time, Joe struggled to use a telephone, so obviously the triage was ineffective. After an appeal (telephoning and writing directly to the head of service), we were bounced to adult services due to an 18-month waiting list and in total ignorance of the 25-year rule (UK). [ECHPs are valid for 25 years and access to "children" services has similar rules]. But we were so desperate we would take any help we could get. Eventually, Joe saw a psychiatrist who provided an additional diagnosis but no way forward. Again, after meetings and conversations with a local manager, Joe was referred to IAPT (CBT therapy). After one session the therapist decided she could not support Joe. I spoke to the manager about where we could go next, but he had absolutely no idea and gave the impression of not caring either. Ironically, they were prepared to offer me and my partner therapy so 'we could cope better'.

During this time, Joe was declining and eventually I discovered who headed up adult mental health services locally. After an exchange of emails, he explained the commissioners had not commissioned suitable services for autistic people. Clearly, he was frustrated with the constraints placed on him by others. However, I learnt from him the name of the commissioner. I never heard from that commissioner, but an underling contacted me with the offer of support from the charity Mind. Mind made a huge difference and that therapist – Magic Emma as we affectionately call her – is still in our lives. She has lived experience.

Another overlooked part of therapy is its duration. Some services provide only six sessions, but this is obviously totally ineffective for autistic people as it may take six sessions just for them to trust the therapist.

Remember some therapists are 'generalists' and will, in my opinion, be totally ineffective at supporting autistic people, let alone helping them. Always ask about lived experience or the general nature of the therapist's clients. The more exposure to autism the better, in my opinion. Please remember that just because someone is called a 'therapist', this doesn't mean they are clinically or academically qualified to act as one.

So, my only advice is to research, network, cajole, threaten and always ask why. No is never an acceptable answer. Always remember your loved one's life may depend on you never giving way.

Apps

Apps have become a fashionable solution to most problems. A wellness app for this, a chatbot for that. While apps may be helpful for providing momentary distractions, they will never solve the issues that need resolving. Linardon *et al* (2024) conducted a meta-analysis of many trials of mindfulness apps and concluded that they may 'help improve symptoms of depression and anxiety to a modest degree'.

We have not personally found any apps to be particularly helpful, and there may be a danger of missing the wood for the trees while your focus is on an app-based solution – could such apps be masking issues that will fester and come back with a vengeance? Joe finds playing games more helpful, and we have over the years bought handheld games consoles, like Nintendo Switch.

Some 'anxiety' reducing apps come with subscriptions and some have monetised content, so caution needs to be exercised if you do want to explore this route. There is nothing lost by trying a few of the apps in their 'free' introductory periods to understand if your loved one will benefit.

CBT

Cognitive behaviour therapy, to give CBT its full name, is a form of talking therapy. It is a common treatment for a range of mental health issues that can impact your life but are not seen as high risk. It is the preferred or first-line treatment for children with social anxiety. The aim of CBT is to teach coping skills for dealing with different problems. Its primary focus is on how a person's thoughts, beliefs and attitudes impact their feelings and actions. For example, you may interpret what someone has said to you in a negative way, and it may cause feelings of melancholy. CBT combines cognitive and behavioural therapy so you can examine how you think, react and behave. In effect, it helps you realise that you are in control of how you respond to others.

Research has shown that it is only mildly effective in treating autistic people unless modified to support autistic thinking patterns. It may be effective in treating a comorbidity but this requires ingenuity on the part of the therapist to untangle the various dynamics at play in autistic clients. While the reasons for the reduced effectiveness of CBT are complex, they can include a reluctance by the person with autism to describe their lives in detail yet again, only to be met with the equivalent of 'You don't look autistic'. Communication issues around accessing therapy, the rigidity of thought, your understanding of the origin of the anxiety, and the finite number of sessions can also cause difficulties.

Repeating the story of their autism journey can be painful for many autistic people. Such retelling can really make matters worse and undo months of painstaking work to build confidence and stability. A lot of the anxiety comes from society and how people react to autistic people and a therapist responding with neurotypical comfort words like 'we are all a little autistic' would not be at all helpful. An open-ended approach to the number of sessions is best, in my opinion, as this would give the person time to get to know the therapist and to become comfortable with the process, while emphasising that your loved one won't be abandoned yet again.

One of the greatest barriers to therapy is how and where it is delivered. For example, a therapist insisting on a telephone triage even though your loved one doesn't use the phone should tell you everything you need to know. Another aspect of CBT that is often overlooked is the need for 'homework' to reinforce the work done in therapy. The concept of homework can be difficult for many autistic people. This is a lesson that has been reinforced often on my journey, and we have struggled with school homework. Insisting on therapy homework can amplify social isolation and cause executive function issues.

A short article (Rogers, 2016) in the BACP journal describes how CBT can be adapted to support and treat autistic people. It is worth reading the article before talking to a therapist. Please remember that a bad therapist can do more harm than good, but a great therapist, like our 'Magic Emma', can be life changing.

ABA/PBS therapy

Applied Behaviour Analysis, or ABA, is controversial. Positive Behaviour Support (PBS) is its more positively named half-sister. It will appear a lot when you search for autism treatments or therapies and you will find numerous positive testimonies and lovely brochures of smiling happy children and happy nurturing parents.

Autism Speaks, a very large American charity, describes ABA as a therapy based on the science of learning and behaviour. The National Autistic Society use PBS in their schools and care homes. The organisation Thinking about Autism organisation has a large list of behaviour-based therapies.

ABA looks at the 'symptoms' your loved one exhibits and attempts to reduce their incidence using rewards, coercion and punishment. Some of the training is very intensive and focuses on taking baby steps. Supporters of the therapy claim that it:

- Increases language and communication skills.
- Improves social skills and attention.
- Decreases the incidence of problem behaviours.

A lot of the therapy is based on positive reinforcement, where you get a reward or some praise for doing something in the required way. This is based on the premise that, over time, because of the reward, the 'behaviour' will become more common.

The remainder of the therapy is based on consequences. Some will interpret this part of the therapy as the punishment part. This part tries to understand why a behaviour occurs and corrects it with a warning and a consequence. An example provided by Autism Speaks involves a teacher allowing a child to play with some toys and then, after a while, asking the child to tidy the toys away. The child ignores the teacher and carries on playing. The consequence is the teacher removes the toys. In this case, the treatment is encouraging the child to ask for more time or to comply. The therapist or teacher does some analysis and develops a plan to modify the errant behaviour.

Sometimes the approach forgets there is more than one road to a goal. It should be remembered that just because a therapist says it is the right way, doesn't make it the right way.

Many years ago, there was a TV show called 'Super Nanny' in which a celebrity would advise parents how to modify bad behaviour in their children – a behaviour-based approach for parents. The lady has successfully helped very many families. We tried some of the lady's suggestions (off the TV) before we knew he was autistic. One concept the lady used was a naughty step for time-outs. This was a disaster because Joe took himself there many times a day because he thought he had done wrong even when he hadn't. We adapted and used reason and kindness instead.

Before embarking on this therapy, pause and do some independent research, talking to autistic people who have had the therapy, and remember that there are always consequences to therapy. Remember that other things, like epilepsy, eating disorders and anxiety, are often bundled with autism. So attempting to correct behaviours around food and mealtimes, for example, may make matters worse and the consequences may not appear for several years.

This section has been difficult to write as I try to not project my prejudice and bias against ABA and PBS. Leaf *et al* (2022) provide an overview of the controversies and benefits of ABA. Shkedy (2021) provides a different viewpoint focused on the long-term consequences of ABA.

Other therapy options

There are many different therapy options available and I would recommend that if you are interested, you do your research and consider what might best make sense for your loved one. I have outlined some options below:

Dialectical therapy

This therapy is based on CBT but is aimed at people who feel emotions intensely. It is adapted from CBT to help clients understand that things that may appear opposite could both be true. An example could simply be your loved one accepting themselves and changing their behaviour accordingly.

It could be useful in learning how to work through waves of depression that could otherwise lead to the pit of no return.

Acceptance and commitment therapy
Acceptance and commitment therapy (ACT) is derived from traditional behaviour therapy and CBT. The therapy teaches not to avoid or deny emotions and instead to accept feelings are appropriate responses that should not prevent them from moving forward in their lives.

Son-Rise therapy
The Son-Rise programme focuses on social interaction through play. The programme focuses on four key areas: eye contact and non-verbal communication, communication, attention span and flexibility. Willams *et al* (2003) and Houghton *et al* (2013) investigated the effectiveness of this therapy. I offer no opinion as I have no experience with this approach, but, as with all therapies, I would advise you do your own extensive research.

Horse-riding therapy
How does horse-riding therapy work, you may ask. No idea, would be my reply. Anecdotally, it appears to make a qualitative difference to autistic and other neuro-divergent children. I have read stories from sources I trust that selectively mute and non-verbal children have begun to talk and other positive changes have followed. Srinivasan *et al* (2018) report improved behaviours and social communication: 'Our review suggested that equine therapy has beneficial effects on behavioural skills and to some extent on social communication in ASD'.

Our Magic Emma uses a combination of many therapies with Joe to keep him settled including Dialectical Therapy and Acceptance and Commitment Therapy, and different parts of each therapy work best for him. She alternates between them automatically.

Alternative medicine
Complementary and alternative medicine presents a popular alternative for autism. Some approaches address some of the core symptoms of autism while others focus on the perceived causes of autism. A detailed discussion of some of these therapies can be found in Brondino *et al* (2015).

The NHS, has a lot of expertise with autism and has compiled an exhaustive list of autism treatments and therapies it does not recommend (NHS, 2024). Please read it with your own independent research and always make an informed choice based on scientific proof of effectiveness.

Chapter 5:
Building resilience

This dynamic journey is unlike any other and it will change and stretch you and your loved one in unsuspected ways. It requires dynamic thinking, constant adjustment and patience, but above all it requires resilience. Resilience is a very important life skill.

Dictionary definitions of resilience talk about a capacity to withstand or to recover quickly from difficulties; a sort of elastic toughness. Think of autism as an elastic band and an egg. The band symbolises the elasticity and the eggshell the toughness, but if you stretch the band too far and it will snap, and if you drop the egg, or knock it, it is forever cracked.

You may think this sounds almost impossible, and is probably like juggling eggs, but the art is to wrap the eggs in many rubber bands, so if one band snaps the rest still protect the egg when it is inevitably dropped.

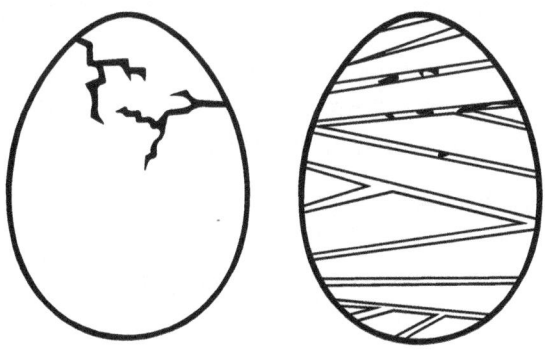

Many self-help books and websites talk about the benefits of positive thinking, self-care, having a support network and working towards goals. Sound advice, but does it work with autism? As you know, many carers and autistic people are lonely and have few genuine friends, which makes it difficult to build a support network. Anxiety, imposter syndrome etc can hinder positive thinking and make it hard to work proactively towards goals.

There are other factors at play, too, that will conspire to hide those elastic bands from us, such as invalidation, assumptions, over-protection, deficits, previous experiences and perfectionism.

As carers, we strive to protect and shield our loved ones from difficulties and failures. We do this because we know the consequences. But in our desire to overprotect, are we wrapping those eggs in so much bubble wrap that the egg disappears? Are we undermining our loved one's independence and self-esteem and increasing their dependence on us?

Society only endures Autism Awareness Day once a year, but every day is an awareness day for autistic people. Each day other people will make assumptions about autistic people's competence to work, have friendships and relationships and be independent. When reinforced, these constant assumptions can become that ever-growing millstone that saps confidence and self-determination. That millstone will snap multiple elastic bands. Previous experiences and failures can colour an autistic person's outlook and desire to try something new or do something again. This is especially true if a previous experience was traumatic.

'Words matter' is something most of us forget about, but words are like water – over time a little stream can erode mountains. Words are the psychological equivalent of that stream. Words and phrases like 'you can't', 'you are unable' etc invalidate a person with their negativity.

Many autistic people have imposter syndrome, in which they think they are not good enough and strive to be perfect. This perfectionism is sometimes mistaken for avoidance or challenging behaviour.

Always remember that resilience is different to independence but is very important on the road to independence. As you focus on increasing your loved one's resilience, please remember it is different to tolerance, but both are closely entwined. And building resilience, like any construction project, needs to start from a place of safety, and that starts with you accepting them as they are.

How

So how do you build up your loved one's resilience? There are many books on the subject, and it may be worth reading a few to find an approach that works for them. In the early years of our journey, we found social stories by Carol Gray (2010) useful and this approach still influences how we do things today. In essence, a social story is just a story that explains the how, what, and why of something. They can cover almost anything and are best framed with a goal in mind.

> Like most parents, we used to sit down with Joe and read stories to and with him, and social stories became part of this. Initially, we wrote small comic strips with stick men to explain things, but as we got better, we developed the story with Joe providing input and tailoring the story to his needs. One story that sticks in my mind was the one we created to prepare Joe for going on holiday for the first after time after diagnosis. Together, we made a book explaining the journey to and through the airport, the flight and the sights and views of our destination. Nowadays we simply discuss things with a focus on different 'what if' scenarios, planning for the best and preparing for the worst. We always discuss mitigation.

Throughout this guide there has been an almost constant theme that *words matter*. I have stressed the importance of kinder and more meaningful words and pausing before responding. Kinder and meaningful words in themselves don't build resilience but they help especially when coupled with a low-arousal approach to parenting. Couple these words with empathy to talk up achievements, however small. You may remember the importance of pebbles on the road to a milestone.

Remember the power of positive reinforcement. We celebrate every pebble and milestone. Really important milestones get permanent reminders, for example a photograph of Joe's beaming face on graduation day is hung in his sensory/safe room. When Joe was in school, we used to celebrate every certificate, prize or positive report with a trifle. We made a routine of celebrating pebbles. It is a practice we still do today when we are proud of something Joe has done.

Like most things with autism, there is only the long road. Building resilience is like building Rome, it is not done in a day, but in many stages. Many autistic people can be overwhelmed if there are too many demands placed on them at once. Because of this, we use lists and routines a lot. Lists help to break more complex tasks down into smaller simpler tasks. Routine helps with those mundane housekeeping and self-care tasks that clutter up everyone's days. Unlike most, we take a flexible approach to most chores as long as they are completed by the appropriate time. For example, Joe is responsible for putting out the rubbish wheelie bins, but we leave him to decide when he puts them out.

Playing to someone's strengths is doing what you know you are good at. Usually, an autistic person's strength revolves around their special interests. This is a powerful way to increase resilience and self-reliance and to improve self-worth. Several years ago, Zak Martin, an autistic man with a PDA profile, was really struggling at senior school and really didn't want to be there anymore. His mum took the brave step of withdrawing him from school and using EOTAS to complete his education via his special interest in power generation. He is now an award-winning autism advocate working on placement with the National Grid because of his extraordinary knowledge.

We have found that practice is helpful. We all know the saying 'practice makes perfect', and building resilience is no different. We practice things in little increments. Over the years, Joe's resilience has increased by encouraging him to take responsibility for himself so he can make his own food, go to the shops and manage his own time without increasing his anxiety. Over the years we have done this slowly, by example. It started by leaving Joe alone in the house while we walked around our neighbourhood for 15 minutes. As Joe realised he could do it, the time increased, and ultimately culminated in a five-day trip to Rome without him (although we did organise considerable support).

Coping mechanisms

Resilience is great, but resilience without support will fail. Coping mechanisms provide the necessary scaffolding to build resilience.

Distraction is a powerful coping tool, and it can be used to boost resilience when things are stressful. Distraction is an abrupt change, where your loved one is distracted by doing something quite different. For example, when Joe was very little, 'Bagpuss' was his go-to distraction, which was replaced with Looney Tunes when he got a little older. A direct consequence of those times is that humour is now one of Joe's best coping mechanisms.

Hobbies are also a useful way of increasing resilience, and they serve as great coping mechanisms. Autistic people often have special interests, and these hyper-hobbies provide an important anchor in their lives. Grove (2018) states that 'Special interests were associated with a number of positive outcomes for autistic adults'.

Deflection is another useful coping mechanism, especially when your loved one is likely to become situationally mute. Deflection is like distraction, but it continues with the current context or theme. This tool is useful when it is difficult to avoid the existing trigger. Joe struggles when things don't always run to time, for example when an aircraft misses it take off slot because of air traffic conditions. Like most people Joe stresses that he will be confined longer than expected in his seat. He talks animatedly about the reasons why our plane should be priority. The longer the wait the more concerned he becomes. To reduce his stress but to keep him talking and avoid a shutdown we deflect him to talk about our aircraft, Boeing and so forth.

This is a skill we have also helped Joe to develop to avoid talking about things he doesn't want to when he is stressed. This is the equivalent of a politician asking a question to avoid asking a question. Joe's equivalence is asking somebody something mundane, like how they are and then smiling and walking off when he has "fine". This approach has been useful when others have taken too much interest in him. This approach is very much dependent on personality and confidence. We have used social stories to create scripts to support this aspect of deflection.

Planning

Building resilience is something that can be planned. As you are aware, 'normal' milestones don't happen unless they are planned. To plan something, you need a goal. Most of our goals are long term and are all focused on increasing Joe's independence so he can live successfully when we are no longer able to support him. Joe's goals are more short term, but require planning to ensure he has the resilience to complete them.

When we have a goal, we work back from it, planning our route from the goal to where we currently are. We think of each pebble that will help us get to that final goal. We focus on the foundations and have a route in mind, but we only cross bridges as and when we come to them.

> A few years ago, Joe decided he wanted more qualifications to increase his chances of finding meaningful work. Joe had a part-time job with a consultancy and developed an interest in IT. Before he took the plunge with a full-time college course, he decided to see if his ideas were feasible, and he was able to complete a course. Joe signed up for an evening class in programming in a nearby town. The logistics of getting Joe back and forth were left to me. I planned my working life around that evening class.
>
> Once he completed the course, Joe's confidence increased and he decided to do a full-time course at our local college. Our first step was to work back, looking at the hoops and hurdles and bridges we may have to build, and decided there were five large pebbles:
>
> - Finance.
> - Getting there.
> - Support in college.
> - Equipment.
> - Focus.
>
> Each pebble required work – the journey to the college is a good example. Joe had four options: his mother and me, a taxi, a train, or a bus. Joe decided to go with the train but was initially unsure. Joe's PA and his mum did the journey with him several times in advance and Joe used an app to buy his tickets. He used the train and an app because they suited his needs best and his resilience to other people.

Feedback

Many services you and your loved one access have complaint/praise or feedback procedures. Please remember that feedback can always include praise. If you don't tell them something works, how will they know?

You need to be aware that complaining sometimes comes with consequences. Hopefully your complaint will result in a better service, but many times you are simply dismissed and ignored. In some extreme cases you may be singled out and your loved one may suffer the consequences.

On my journey, I have encountered many parents who have been called 'names' by people working in the services they have complained about. Some even keep dossiers on you and track your posts on social media. We have been branded as 'awkward' by LA officers and one once described us as 'ignorant and pushy' to our faces. I am aware that is mild in comparison to the abuse many have endured, but some of the gentlest people I know have been called intimidating and their loved ones have suffered the consequences of their feedback.

Complaining about mental health services is difficult. It is probably quicker to just write to the top dog rather than go through the approved procedures. We tried the approved approach once and got nowhere, but after complaining to the head of service we got some access.

Complaining, I have realised much too late, requires precision, persistence and consistency. Precision in identifying the appropriate person your feedback must reach and what or who you are providing feedback on. Persistence, because you must constantly cajole, remind, and threaten to get any outcome. Consistency in how you approach the issue, whether you pull in items of law and statutory duty etc.

Praise is important because it may help an organisation evolve into one that is more tolerant and supportive. When you offer praise, you may encounter jealousy and pettiness from many. Many years ago, I tried to nominate an extraordinary SENCO for an award in the Queen's Birthday Honours. I had support from several parents and the school's senior management but there was no support from the local government. Despite my efforts and the school's, the Cabinet Office would not consider the request.

Some carers have used the media to force change. These individuals are braver than I am. When you provide feedback, always have an end goal in mind. Remember, you don't control the narrative when the media is involved.

A dear friend of mine has made several complaints about his LA:

> *'I learnt a lot from that: the amount of time, the way the LA start to treat you and also that every time someone makes an official complaint, it stays on record no matter what stage the complaint is closed at'. It's important to remember that this process is not free from stress and sometimes there will be consequences in how LA officers will treat you.*

When you complain about your LA formally, always write to them to begin the process. There are usually two stages. In the first stage, your complaint will be investigated by people close to the service or people you are complaining about. In the second stage, your complaint will be looked at by someone not connected to the service. If you are not satisfied with the response, you can further complain to the Local Government Ombudsman (LGO). The IPSEA charity has sample letters that you may find helpful if you decide to formally complain.

Chapter 6:
Lived experience

Most social media forums, whether Facebook, Twitter, or any of the others, are full of negative stories about autism. Many want instant fixes to complex issues and many dwell on how hard life is. Some even question what they have done to deserve this journey. There are rarely any positive stories about autism or their loved ones.

This section is about positives and successes, but please forget how you personally measure success. Success for some of these people could be as a simple as getting up in the morning or still being here. Each of these people have considerable resilience to just survive what may appear to be never ending curve balls. Simon describes this as "Surviving out of Spite".

The people in this section have appeared throughout this guide to illustrate key points or to present a different view of autism. Some of these people are included under pseudonyms and some parts of their journey have been omitted or reordered to ensure anonymity.

Each of these profiles clearly show with autism there are no short cuts just the long road. A road where your mindset is the most important trait you have. A growth mindset that enables you to prosper in your own unique way and be able to support those reliant on you no matter what comes.

Luke

This is the story of Luke, an autistic teenager who also happens to have epilepsy. Luke's autism appeared after his epilepsy. Luke lives with his mum and two siblings. Luke's siblings are very supportive of him, despite being younger. They look out for their big brother.

Luke was a bright child who did well in primary school until he started 'daydreaming'. His teachers started to complain that he was always daydreaming and was becoming lazy. His mum also noticed Luke was quieter at home and reached out to her GP, but she was fobbed off. She persisted with the GP, but nothing changed.

One day, she was told to collect him from school. She thought they'd had enough of his daydreaming but when arrived she noticed Luke was ashen and listless and was clearly in need of medical attention. The school also appeared to be in a hurry to get him off the premises.

She quickly arranged for his siblings to be collected by grandparents while she took Luke to the GP. As expected, the GP's receptionist said there were no appointments, and no medical staff were available to see him. She was left with no choice but to take Luke to A&E.

At A&E Luke was triaged by a nurse who was none the wiser about what was up, but a junior doctor, with lived experience, knew. Luke's mum was shocked. No one had hinted at epilepsy before. The doctor explained that the 'daydreaming' was caused by very frequent micro-seizures and he was having a 'full' seizure at that moment.

Over time, Luke stabilised as his mum and clinicians worked to get the right drug regimen to manage the epilepsy. His mum ensured everyone had epilepsy training and everywhere Luke went there was always a spare 'epi' pen. At first, the school were reluctant to have the training, but his mum persisted, and she explained that she couldn't always be available to collect him.

Despite the training, the school always summoned his mum at the slightest hint of a full seizure. After serval months, Luke's teachers started to complain again, saying that he was rude and wouldn't always listen. He was 'too logical', apparently. Mum had also noticed that Luke's personality had changed. He was more matter-of-fact and direct. Both the school and his mum thought it could be a side effect of the medication.

She went to the GP and was again fobbed off. She tried the assigned epileptic nurse who was more helpful and referred Luke to see an SLT therapist. Because of the long wait times, she persisted with the GP and was eventually passed to a paediatrician who knew how to help. The paediatrician explained that Luke was autistic.

After Luke's mum informed the school of the autism, things changed. Everything seemed to be too much for them. Epilepsy and autism are a complicated bundle. Luke started to get anxious about things, with sudden mood swings, and he lost considerable self-confidence.

His mum asked CAHMS for help, but they just blamed autism or epilepsy for the anxiety. When she eventually got on the CAHMS waiting list, she was told the wait was about 18 months. She asked the school and the local authority if they could do anything to support Luke and was told she could 'trust' them.

After many years of little support (except from family) Luke's mum lost it. She asked for a statutory assessment and got the usual local authority 'doesn't meet the threshold' run around. She persisted but was ignored. Meanwhile, Luke went to the local comprehensive school. Apparently, they were good with autism and mum could trust them.

After a few weeks, however, it was evident that they didn't get autism at all and Luke had very little support in class. His mum was constantly at the school demanding support and she repeatedly asked that they apply for a Statement. After Luke was hospitalised by a bully for the third time, his mum applied for a statutory assessment herself. The LA declined.

Around this time, Luke's paternal grandfather retired and started supporting his mum in meetings. Luke's grandfather is a self-made man, a successful local builder, and a person who you rarely said no to.

Unknown to his mum, Luke's grandfather arranged a face-to-face meeting with the officer who said no. At the meeting, he listened patiently and made notes and after a meeting spoke to a solicitor who owed him a favour. Luke's mum and grandfather had a long chat with the solicitor and appealed the decision. A Statement of educational need soon followed. It had only taken nine years to get to this point.

The Statement enabled his mum to move Luke to a more supportive and suitable school. Luke thrived at that school, and he is now at technical college learning to be a chef.

Persistence and knowledge of the law pay.

Simon

Simon is a late-diagnosed adult with an additional diagnosis of schizoid-affective disorder. Simon's autism was noticed when his life took a bad turn.

Simon was a quiet lad in school. He studied hard, went to a good university, and graduated with an Honours Degree in computer science. As expected, he quickly found meaningful employment and a few years later met someone he thought would be his lifelong partner. After a few years, Simon and his partner emigrated to Australia.

While in Australia, Simon's life started to unravel. Most people think Australia is the same as the UK but with sunshine, but the culture and social rules are subtly quite different. Simon struggled to acclimatise to the different culture and social rules and, as a result, his relationship started to break down. After a few years of constant struggling with depression and other things, Simon was diagnosed with a schizoaffective disorder and bipolar. Initially, this was confusing, but with time everything started to make sense, but by now his relationship had fallen apart.

Simon decided to start afresh by returning to the UK. He returned to his lifelong rock and confidante – his beloved mum. Simon's life steadied and he found a job and began another relationship. After a while, Simon started hearing voices and was sectioned for his own safety. During his stay in hospital, Simon was diagnosed with autism but after a while he was able to resume his old life. And then, just as things were starting to look up for him, his beloved mum died causing Simon to relapse.

Living with someone with a mental illness can put an immense strain on any relationship, and during Simon's latest stay in a mental health hospital, his partner ended the relationship and made him homeless overnight. Despite recovering from his relapse, Simon was further (voluntarily) detained until appropriate accommodation could be found for him. Eventually, his local authority found Simon a room in a hotel while they searched for a more permanent appropriate home.

Simon still has his struggles but has written about his experiences of the UK mental health system, educates people about autism and mental health issues on social media, and has developed a few apps to help autistic adults navigate a hostile world.

If you consider that Simon has had to start his life from zero three times, he has done remarkably well considering the curve balls he has been pitched. We should also celebrate Simon's humanity and his desire to educate people by sharing his daily struggles. His motto remains to "Survive out of spite".

Keith Ridley

Keith Ridley is a non-verbal autistic gentleman with a profound learning disability. He was diagnosed at 16. He lives with his parents and autistic sister. He suffers from IBS and communicates by pointing, tapping people, and taking people to what he wants. He makes distinct noises to express his needs.

Only those who know him understand his unique style of communication. In recent years he was dropped from local authority day services. Covid lockdowns seriously impacted his mental health. Assessing his mental health and other needs is quite difficult without his family. His family is his only advocate.

Keith is anxious around strangers. If there are strangers in the home he becomes very anxious and can rapidly become agitated. This impacts family life considerably and limits the time available for people visiting or tradesmen carried out work. This requires considerable effort to ensure any is done when Keith is in Respite or at his day centre.

Last year, he endured a two-week stay in hospital following an accident at his Day Care Centre. He was almost in a permanent state of distress because most medical staff ignored the advice of his family.

Over the years his family have constantly had to be vigilant to ensure he kept any services that support his unique needs. Covid was exceptionally difficult for the family as all services closed. Following Covid, there a struggle to regain access to services.

Recently, he has transferred to CHC funding from LA funded services. His family reports that CHC support just 'gets it' without argument or confrontation. His family reports that he is content.

Graham

Graham is a dear friend. He is an autistic carer who cares for his lovely wife and his autistic son. Graham has been working with his local authority to improve services by increasing understanding. The following describes Graham's journey in his own words.

> *Graham is a semi-retired unpaid carer. He cares for his wife, who has had CP since birth and who is not very mobile, and his autistic son, aged 25.*
>
> *Graham believes he is autistic having been screened and having completed several online tools, including AQ-10. Graham is currently waiting on an adult diagnostic pathway. The expected wait is four years. Graham has been diagnosed as ADHD, more specifically ADD, and has Executive Dysfunction.*
>
> *Graham has always thought that he was different to many people and was brought up in a service family background, father was in the RAF, he was constantly on the move. While this meant that he spent 3 years in Cyprus as a teenager, a lot longer than a fortnight holiday, it has meant that Graham has no friends from his childhood.*
>
> *Graham had thought that he was a bit shy and prone to procrastination and intermittent poor mental health. He now realises that events in his past can be explained by neurodivergence.*
>
> *This is a story of Graham's career, his on-going struggle to access support for his loved ones and his extraordinary advocacy to make things easier for those that follow him.*
>
> *When Graham's son was diagnosed with Asperger's at the age of 10 he made an assumption that the Council and the schools would look after his son. Graham attended the annual review meetings and continued with his assumptions. Sadly, that assumption was not validated by events and Graham realised that the Council and schools had not*

provided the care and support that his son really needed. Graham will remember that assumption and the problems that it created for his son until the day he dies.

Graham found out that complaints against a Council must be submitted within one year and so he started to review what the law said about Autism. This was relevant to his son and many other autistic people. Reading up on the Autism Act, very short, and the accompanying Strategies and Statutory Guidance, Graham soon realised that many elements of these were not available on his Council's website. He contacted the head of both Adult and Children's Services to ask how they had implemented the Strategy and Statutory Guidance and received a letter acknowledging his requests 56 days after he wrote them. They must have been delayed by the postal strike, wrote the Council. They were dropped in the letter box at the front of the Council's building. It has been a struggle to get any contact with the Council, until they recently contacted people through a local charity, TalkBack. Graham is persevering with his approaches to the Council.

In a recent book, entitled Autism and the Law Navigating a legal Minefield (Pavilion, 2024), *the author identifies that many Councils have been put in an impossible position of providing adult service and maintaining a balanced budget while the funding from Government has steadily decreased. So his Councils, like many others, cannot provide the care that the law requires. With this in mind, Graham continues to request care and help for himself and his son. If the Council social worker makes an error or does not follow the Council's procedures, and so the law, the social worker responds by saying that the only option available to Graham is to make a formal complaint.*

Graham's son is autistic and suffer from poor mental health and low self-esteem. His son has been referred to NHS mental health services who contacted Graham initially to confirm the referral and to admit that the person knows nothing about Autism. Graham and his son wait for the next approach, not knowing when that will be or from whom.

Graham is very concerned about his son's future especially as he does not understand 'officialdom' and is unlikely to be able to cope without Graham. His son sees politicians as people who sit behind big oak desks in an office in London.

> In researching the law about autism, Graham has realised that
> he can help others. His current conundrum is how that can be
> achieved. Pointing someone to a piece of law, written in legalise
> barely understood by lawyers, does not help, nor does showing
> someone the detailed procedures used by his Council. The major
> problem with the law in the UK at the moment is that some
> people do not follow or abide by it; these are constrained by cost
> and management pressures. So Graham is currently preparing
> summaries of the law for others to use.
>
> Graham recognises that he is not the first person to take on this
> mammoth task and there are many charities that have produced
> some very good guides and advice. Most are in specific areas and are
> not always connected to the next piece of advice.
>
> If you meet one autistic person, you have met one autistic person.
> By documenting their lives and how they have overcome problems
> we all face, such as this book, ore people can better understand the
> problems they have or may face.

Graham's basic advice to all readers is to write your lived experience down and share it with others.

Leanne and Jordan

Leanne is a disabled carer who cares for her autistic adult son Jordan. Jordan has also has epilepsy, IBS, hydrocephalus and a learning disability. Jordan is very sensitive to smells and at times they can make him nauseous. Jordan is situational mute bordering on non-verbal because of low muscle tone. Within his family he can be very talkative and loves sharing details of his day. Jordan attends a private day centre most weekdays and for respite.

Leanne has multiple disabilities including anxiety, probable autism and ADHD (from a private consultation). Leanne also has mobility issues and relies on a mobility scooter.

Leanne started her own travel agency in 2021 to fit around her unique family, but ideally Leanne would prefer the structure of working for a company in a travel agency shop. All attempts to work for a travel company have been met with the "no experience" excuse. Obviously, this is an excuse given the 20 years plus experience and extensive travel qualifications Leanne has.

Jordan's school life made holding down a job difficult due to schools constantly telephoning Leanne to collect Jordan from school when he had an IBS or sensory related incident. Some schools always insisted that Jordan was kept home for a day or two after an incident.

Interestingly whilst Leanne has had the usual battles with her LA, she looks at the outcomes as being lucky and knowing beforehand what her family was entitled to. However, it has not always been straight forward, and to even gain respite was difficult because of a social worker who didn't get it. To get respite care Leanne had to register Jordan on the "Child in need" register using the Section 17 of the Children Act 1989.

One anecdote Leanne shared was about respite; when Jordan was attending the local college and was in respite the LA expected Leanne to still take Jordan to and from college. The LA struggled to understand that Jordan would struggle with the lack of continuity and that it made the respite almost worthless to Leanne in terms of real down time.

Leanne has strong opinions about the DWP that are best described as, "if your face fits it works but if it doesn't you get fobbed off". One of the plus sides of dealing with the DWP was meeting a learning disability nurse who had previously supported the family. The same nurse assessed Jordan when he transferred to PIP. Leanne is not looking forward when Jordan transfers from ESA to Universal Credit.

Like most unpaid carers and disabled people Leanne and Jordan have met with considerable discrimination. Leanne says people just don't listen or open their eyes. Leanne says people really don't get non-verbal people and take their "frustration" out on the non-verbal person.

One anecdote shared was about a holiday in Benidorm when two mature ladies constantly complained that the family had an accessible room on the ground floor whilst they had to make do with a room on upper storey accessible by lift.

Leanne's advice is understand "life is good" and make "your luck by knowing the right information first".

Chapter 6: Lived experience

Paul Ridley

Paul Ridley is a dear friend. He is a champion for carers and the rights of autistic people, especially those who are nonverbal and have learning disabilities. Paul has probably neuro-divergent traits but has no interest in pursuing a diagnosis. His special interest is American Football, and his team is Minnesota Vikings.

Paul originates form Southend and admits to being a "Jack the lad" before he met his wife, Sarah. After meeting Sarah, he trained as a chef and ended up managing (and head chef) a highly respected local restaurant.

Paul and Sarah have two children who are both autistic. "C" their daughter was diagnosed with Asperger's Syndrome. She manages to hold down a job with a very large company. Keith their youngest, above, is non-verbal with profound and complex needs.

Paul's journey with autism spans over 3 decades and is full of battles with professionals, the local authority, Ombudsmen, and politicians who don't listen. Paul has asked questions of Prime Ministers face to face. Paul has that growth mindset discussed earlier. Paul labels his mindset as his intimidator's mode.

Over the years Paul has accumulated considerable lived experience of both "ends of the spectrum". Recently, following the more recent battles with his local authority and our NHS Paul has started sharing that information with professionals in his LA and NHS. He has created a series of videos focusing on non-verbal autism with Stoke Mandeville Hospital to complement the Oliver McGowan Mandatory training.

Over the years Paul has advocated for both his children. An example of this was intervening when a new manager at "C"'s employer was not making reasonable adjustments. "C" does her job as she always has and is always praised at every appraisal for her attention to detail and focus. The new manager wanted "C" to do things his way. This caused a considerable period of burnout from excessive masking. Paul politely intervened and educated the manager about autism. More recently when his LA could no longer meet Keith's needs, he single handily found the Care Facility that provides day and respite care for the family.

Paul is worried about the future for both his children. He is worried about the implication of welfare changes and who will care for and advocate and care for his children when he and Sarah are no longer here.

Over the years Paul has struggled with his mental and physical health from this stress of the near constant attritional battles with local and central government agencies. Despite this he always tries to be positive.

Andreas

Andreas is a very well-educated unpaid carer. Andreas works in scientific research. In primary school Andrea's parents were told he would amount to nothing, but the teacher considerably underestimated Andreas's ability. The teachers associated social skills with outcomes.

When transferring to senior school Andreas was placed in the bottom most set with "remedial" and learning-disabled children. Within a week he was in the academic top set. However, he still struggled with social interaction and how others perceived him. After graduating from one of the best universities in the UK, he worked for a company that required considerable social skills to progress, but he was always called on in his area to do the most complex solutions. In frustration with progress, he left and returned to university where he gained 3 higher degrees in very complex subjects.

After a few failed relationships he began to wonder if there was something "wrong" with him. During this time, he saw a psychiatrist to see what was "wrong". The Psychiatrist said he was cognitive very able and was "just shy".

Following university he had a period of unemployment, he just couldn't see to get passed the interviews. Finally, he was luckily with another university assisting in complex research. During this time, he met his wife, who is his guiding light or "Northern Star". Andrea's wife is neurodivergent. All of the children are neurodivergent. He still struggles with social skills but is very glad to have found someone who accepts and appreciates him as he is, "warts and all" so to speak.

One of the children is autistic and after many years Andreas' has realised, he is probably autistic. He has no plans to be diagnosed.

The focus and pattern recognition that come with autism have been key to Andreas' continuing technical employment. The focus and pattern recognition have been useful in ensuring all the children have had appropriate support in school and beyond.

Like most carer's there was the usual attritional trench warfare with local and central government over SEN and access to services. The focus and in-built directness ensured that growth mindset described earlier was already present. It just needed polishing to remove the sharper edges.

Over the years, like most unpaid carers, Andreas has struggled with his mental health because of the stress of dealing with government. Several years ago, he realised that his perceptions of other people not appreciating him was their problem rather than his. This realisation helped his mental health become more resilient.

Chapter 7:
Conclusion

When you start a journey with autism it can feel like basic training in the Army at times; you are always running to keep up. Everything is unfamiliar, and you are stretched and stressed in ways you never thought possible. I hope this guide will help you to run a little slower and help you to realise that you are not alone, and the whole extended community is in your squad supporting and cheering you on.

Autism is complicated, and more so when there is a bundle. Your experience of it may evolve and it keeps you on your toes, and much of the experience is unseen by many people. You have experienced the system and how it sees you and your loved ones. At times it may be hard, but pause and remember: when you get it right, it is funny and joyous and wonderful. When you have a meaningful conversation, the twists of logic, the pattern recognition and sideways perspectives can make everything fun and sometimes even hilarious. Remember, it's never boring!

Throughout this guide I have tried to show that autistic people are just like everyone else, and only want to have a full life like everyone else. I hope I have shown that many of the assumptions and stereotypes surrounding autism are probably baseless, and the truth is in the opposites, like empathy for example; you may recall most autistic people have too much empathy.

The takeaways

There are ten takeaways I want you to remember:

1. Autism does not have to be not scary. Ignorance, indifference, and intolerance make it scary.
2. The only official friend you have is the law. The law trumps policy, opinions, and procedures. Understand the difference between a statutory duty and a guideline.
3. Lived experience makes you an expert. The NHS classes you as an "Expert by Experience", so always remember that you know your loved one better than any professional, assessor or teacher.
4. Anything is possible. Although the journey may be longer, the outcome is always the same. If your loved one has the potential, embrace and enable it.
5. Remember that milestones are loose guidelines. Try not to compare your loved one with someone else's child.
6. Celebrate every pebble and party like there is no tomorrow at every milestone. Think of the joy of a friend when his non-verbal son said "Dad" for the first time. You will have plenty of these moments.
7. If you don't have an answer or solution, ask the extended autistic community. An autistic person or unpaid carer will have an answer for what you need.
8. The system won't tell you everything you are entitled to. Always appeal every decision that goes against your instincts.
9. DEFCON is important. Develop routines and build a safe place to help your loved one to "de-people" and unwind. Over time, this pays dividends.
10. Find time for you, even if it is only 'snatched time'.

That Mindset

A constant theme throughout this guide has been a growth mindset, where you learn from and adapt to every situation. My journey is only possible because I stand on the shoulders of giants: the autistic people and parents who have prepared the road for me. Always listen and learn, but always make your own decisions because only you and your loved one know how fast to travel on that road.

Whilst this journey may sometimes feel like warfare, hopefully I have shown you how to use that mindset to prepare and plan for each of the battles you face. Remember to do your "haka" to get that game face on and, always whoop, punch the air, or do your little dance to celebrate each time you win, no matter how small..

The last part of that mindset is dealing with toxic people. Mark Twain, a favourite of mine, once said, "Never argue with stupid people, they will drag you down to their level and then beat you with experience". In reality, this means that you will never explain or rationalise anything to them. So simply go around, or avoid them altogether. You'll feel the better for it.

You may recall that I use hats to symbolise the many roles I have do to make this journey possible. A vital part of this analogy is my hat stand, where some days I just hang my hats. A day with no hats in order to allow for some down time is something you should never feel guilty about.
If you need a duvet day, have one, because that day will make a huge difference to your mindset and will enable you to do what you need to do, when you need to do it.

Final words

You are on your own unique journey, as we all are, but I hope this guide has helped to show that you are not alone. I hope this guide has helped to show that you and your loved one can have fun-filled and rich lives, and in doing so you will learn what really matters; you and yours.

My final words to you are simple but need to be said loudly:

YOU ARE DOING A FANTASTIC JOB!

Glossary

ABA	Applied Behaviour Analysis
ASD	Autism Spectrum Disorder
BPD	Bipolar Disorder
CAMHS	Child and Adolescent Mental Health Service
CBT	Cognitive Behaviour Therapy
CDC	Center for Disease Control
DSM	Diagnostic and Statistical Manual of Mental Health Disorders
DWP	Department for Works and Pensions
EHCP	Education and Health Care Plan
GP	General Practitioner
ICD	International Classification of Diseases
LD	Learning Disabilities
MH	Mental Health
MHA	Mental Health Act
NAS	National Autistic Society
NHS	National Health Service
PA	Personal Assistant
PACE	Police and Criminal Evidence
PBS	Positive Behaviour Support
SEN	Special Educational Needs
SENCO	Special Educational Needs Coordinator
WHO	World Health Organization

References

Barber C (2018) Loneliness and mental health. *British Journal of Mental Health Nursing* **7** (5) 209-214.

Badshah N (2023) British teenager behind GTA 6 hack receives indefinite hospital order. *The Guardian*. Available at: www.theguardian.com/uk-news/2023/dec/21/british-teenager-behind-gta-6-hack-receives-indefinite-hospital-order (accessed May 2024).

Bravo-Benítez J, Pérez-Marfil MN, Román-Alegre B, Cruz-Quintana F (2019) Grief Experiences in Family Caregivers of Children with Autism Spectrum Disorder (ASD). *Int J Environ Res Public Health* **16** (23) 4821.

Bernier R, Mao A, and Yen J (2010) Psychopathology, families, and culture: autism. *Child Adolesc Psychiatric Clin N Am* **19** (2010) 855–867.

Bettelheim B (1967) *The Empty Fortress: Infantile autism and the birth of the self*. New York: The Free Press.

Brause D (2024) *When Therapy Harms Neurodivergent Clients* [online]. *Psychology Today*, March 2024. Available at: www.psychologytoday.com/intl/blog/psychology-meets-neurodiversity/202402/when-therapy-harms-neurodivergent-clients (accessed May 2024).

Brede J, Cage E, Trott J, Palmer L, Smith A, L, Mandy W, Russell A (2022) 'We Have to Try to Find a Way, a Clinical Bridge' – autistic adults' experience of accessing and receiving support for mental health difficulties: A systematic review and thematic meta-synthesis. *Clinical Psychology Review* **93** https://doi.org/10.1016/j.cpr.2022.102131.

Britannica (2024) *Temple Grandin* [online]. Available at: www.britannica.com/biography/Temple-Grandin (accessed May 2024).

Brondino N, Fusar-Poli L, Rocchetti M, Provenzani U, Barale F, Politi P (2015) Complementary and Alternative Therapies for Autism Spectrum Disorder. *Evid Based Complement Alternat Med.* 2015:258589. https://doi.org/10.1155/2015/258589.

Burrows D, Lyttleton-Smith J, Sheehan L and Jones S (2021) *Voices of carers during the COVID-19 pandemic: messages for the future of unpaid caring in Wales* [online]. Cardiff University. Available at: https://phw.nhs.wales/publications/publications1/voices-of-carers-during-the-covid-19-pandemic-messages-for-the-future-of-unpaid-caring-in-wales (accessed May 2024).

Carers UK (2024) *Your Rights in Work* [online]. Available at: www.carersuk.org/media/uarbiuje/your-rights-in-work-september-2022.pdf (accessed May 2024).

CDC (2023) *Prevalence and Characteristics of Autism Spectrum Disorder Among Children Aged 8 Years* [online]. CDC. Available at: www.cdc.gov/mmwr/volumes/72/ss/ss7202a1.htm?s_cid=ss7202a1_w (accessed May 2024).

Churchard A, Ryder M, Greenhill A, and Mandy W (2019) The prevalence of autistic traits in a homeless population. *Autism* **23** (3) 665-676.

J SE, Constable HL and Mullally SL (2023) 'School distress and the school attendance crisis: a story dominated by neurodivergence and unmet need'. *Front. Psychiatry* 14:1237052. https://doi.org/10.3389/fpsyt.2023.1237052.

Crowell A, Keluskar J and Gorecki A (2019) Parenting behavior and the development of children with autism spectrum disorder. *Comprehensive Psychiatry* **90** 21-29.

Cullen AM, Lindsay G (2019) Special educational needs: understanding drivers of complaints and disagreements in the English system. *Front. Educ. Sec. Special Educational Needs* **4** https://doi.org/10.3389/feduc.2019.00077.

Czech, H (2018) Hans Asperger, National Socialism, and 'race hygiene' in Nazi-era Vienna. *Molecular Autism* **9** (29).

Davies J, Cooper K, Killick E, Sam E, Healy M, Thompson G, Mandy W, Redmayne B and Crane L (2024) Autistic identity: A systematic review of quantitative research. *Autism Research*. https://doi.org/10.1002/aur.3105.

Dept of Health (2023) *Autism Statistics* [online]. Available at: www.health-ni.gov.uk/articles/autism-statistics (accessed May 2024).

Dixon E (2021) *Autism and Maternal Stress: Some parents of children with autism can experience trauma-related symptomology* [online]. Psychology Today. Available at: www.psychologytoday.com/gb/blog/the-flourishing-family/202109/autism-and-maternal-stress (accessed May 2024).

Fitzpatrick M (2005) Why can't the *Daily Mail* eat humble pie over MMR? *BMJ* **331** 1148 https://doi.org/10.1136/bmj.331.7525.1148.

Garrett K and Abreu L (2023) *Autism: Overview of policy and services* [online]. House of Common Library. Available at: https://commonslibrary.parliament.uk/research-briefings/cbp-7172/ (accessed May 2024).

Garratt E and Flaherty J (2021) 'There's nothing I can do to stop it': homelessness among autistic people in a British city. *Disability & Society* **38** (9) 1558–1584.

Gerrard RB, "There is no autism epidemic, but there is an autism diagnosis epidemic", Stat, Feb 2022. https://www.statsnews.com/2022/02/10/theres-no-autism-epidemic-but-there-is an autism-diagnosis-epidemic/

Gesi C, Migliarese G, Torriero S, Capellazzi M, Omboni AC, Cerveri G and Mencacci C (2021) Gender Differences in Misdiagnosis and Delayed Diagnosis among Adults with Autism Spectrum Disorder with No Language or Intellectual Disability. *Brain Sciences* **11** (7) 912.

Gray, C. (2010) *The New Social Story Book*. Future Horizons.

Griffiths S, Allison C, Kenny R, Holt R, Smith P and Baron-Cohen S (2018) The Vulnerability Experiences Quotient (VEQ): A study of vulnerability, mental health and life satisfaction in autistic adults. *Autism Research* **(12)** 1516–1528.

Harris J (2024) As councils crumble, a new scapegoat has been found: the parents of disabled and vulnerable children. *The Guardian*, January 7th. Available at: www.theguardian.com/commentisfree/2024/jan/07/councils-scapegoat-parents-disabled-vulnerable-children-support (accessed May 2024).

HM Government (2024), "Access to Work", https://www.gov.uk/access-to-work, accessed July 2024.

Houghton K, Schuchard J, Lewis C and Thompson C (2013) Promoting child-initiated social-communication in children with autism: Son-Rise Program intervention effects. *Journal of Communication Disorders* **46** (5–6) 495-506, ISSN 0021-9924.

Hours C, Recasens C, and Baleyte J (2022) ASD and ADHD Comorbidity: What Are We Talking About? Front. Psychiatry 13 https://doi.org/10.3389/fpsyt.2022.837424.

Jones EK and Orchard V (2024) Neurodiversity and disability: what is at stake? *Medical Humanities*. Https://doi.org/10.1136/medhum-2023-012808.

Kentrou V, Livingston L, Grove R, Hoekstar R and Begeer S (2024) Perceived misdiagnosis of psychiatoric conditions in autistic adults. *The Lancet* **71** https://doi.org/10.1016/j.eclinm.2024.102586.

Kim H (2012) Autism across cultures: rethinking autism. *Disability & Society* **27** (4) 535-545 https://doi.org/10.1080/09687599.2012.659463

Leaf JB, Cihon JH, Leaf R, McEachin J, Liu N, Russell N, Unumb L, Shapiro S and Khosrowshahi D (2022) Concerns About ABA-Based Intervention: An Evaluation and Recommendations. *J Autism Dev Disord* **52** (6) 2838-2853.

Linardon J, Messer M, Goldberg S, Fuller-Tyszkiewicz M (2024) The efficacy of mindfulness apps on symptoms of depression and anxiety: An updated meta-analysis of randomized controlled trials. *Clinical Psychology Review* **107**.

Lord C, Charman T, Havdahl A, Carbone P, Anagnostou E, Boyd B, Carr T, de Vries P, Dissanayake C, Divan G, Freitag C, Gotelli M, Kasari C, Knapp M, Mundy P and Plank A (2022) The Lancet Commission on the future of care and clinical research in autism. *The Lancet*.

Mandy W, Midouhas E, Hosozawa M, Cable N, Sacker A and Flouri E (2022) Mental health and social difficulties of late-diagnosed autistic children, across childhood and adolescence 2022, *Journal of Child Psychology and Psychiatry* **63** (11) pp1405-1414.

References

Murray, D (2020) Monotropism: An Interest-Based Account of Autism. In: Volkmar, F. (eds) *Encyclopedia of Autism Spectrum Disorders*. Springer, New York, NY. https://doi.org/10.1007/978-1-4614-6435-8_102269-2

NAAN (2019) *There to Help 2* [online]. Available at: www.appropriateadult.org.uk/ (accessed May 2024).

NAS, Mind (2023) *Good Practice Guide* [online]. Available at: https://s2.chorus-mk.thirdlight.com/file/24/asDKIN9as.klK7easFDsalAzTC/NAS-Good-Practice-Guide-A4.pdf (accessed May 2024).

National Academies of Sciences, Engineering, and Medicine (2020) 'Social Isolation and Loneliness in Older Adults: Opportunities for the Health Care System'. Washington, DC: The National Academies Press. https://doi.org/10.17226/25663.

Newell V, Phillips L, Jones C *et al* (2023) A systematic review and meta-analysis of suicidality in autistic and possibly autistic people without co-occurring intellectual disability. *Molecular Autism* **14** 12 (2023). https://doi.org/10.1186/s13229-023-00544-7.

NHS (2024) *Treatments that are not recommended for autism* [online]. www.nhs.uk/conditions/autism/autism-and-everyday-life/treatments-that-are-not-recommended-for-autism/ (accessed May 2024).

O'Connel H and Fizgerald M (2014) Did Alan Turing have Asperger syndrome? *Irish Journal of Psycholgical Medicine*. Available at: www.cambridge.org/core/journals/irish-journal-of-psychological-medicine/article/abs/did-alan-turing-have-aspergers-syndrome/4A888BE5320676AE413094B85EFBEF79 (accessed May 2024).

O'Nions E, Petersen I, Buckman JEJ, Charlton R, Cooper C, Corbett A, Happé F, Manthorpe J, Richards M, Saunders R, Zanker C, Mandy W and Stott J (2023) Autism in England: assessing underdiagnosis in a population-based cohort study of prospectively collected primary care data. *Lancet Reg Health Eur.* **3** 29:100626. https://doi.org/10.1016/j.lanepe.2023.100626.

Palumbo Jennifer J (2022) Why An Autism Diagnosis Is Not A Label But A Roadmap. *Forbes*. Available at: www.forbes.com/sites/jenniferpalumbo/2022/04/25/why-an-autism-diagnosis-is-not-a-label-but-a-roadmap/ (accessed May 2024).

Parliament (2020) *Support for children with special educational needs and disabilities, Committee for Public Accounts* [online]. Available at: https://publications.parliament.uk/pa/cm5801/cmselect/cmpubacc/85/85.pdf (accessed May 2024).

Parliament (2022) *Draft Mental Health Bill 2022 Joint Committee report* [online]. Available at: https://publications.parliament.uk/pa/jt5803/jtselect/jtmentalhealth/696/report.html#heading-5 (accessed May 2024).

Penot J (2023) *The Problem of Loneliness for People With Autism* [online]. Psychology Today. Available at: www.psychologytoday.com/gb/blog/the-forgotten-women/202303/the-problem-of-loneliness-for-people-with-autism (accessed May 2024).

Petrillo M, Bennet M and Price G (2022) *Cycles of Caring* [online]. Available at: https://centreforcare.ac.uk/updates/2022/11/new-report-carers-rights-day-2022/ (accessed May 2024).

Praslova L (2021) *Autism Doesn't Hold People Back at Work: Discrimination Does* [online]. Harvard Business Review. Available at: https://hbr.org/2021/12/autism-doesnt-hold-people-back-at-work-discrimination-does (accessed May 2024).

Pham HH, Sandberg N, Trinkl J and Thayer J (2022) Racial and Ethnic Differences in Rates and Age of Diagnosis of Autism Spectrum Disorder. *JAMA Netw Open* **5** (10) e2239604. https://doi.org/10.1001/jamanetworkopen.2022.39604.

Purlang A (2021) *It's Time To Stop Even Casually Misusing Disability Words* [online]. Forbes. Available at: www.forbes.com/sites/andrewpulrang/2021/02/20/its-time-to-stop-even-casually-misusing-disability-words/ (accessed May 2024).

Ribolsi M (2022) Recognizing Psychosis in Autism Spectrum Disorder. *Front. Psychiatry* **13** https://doi.org/10.3389/fpsyt.2022.768586

Robinson JL, Nations L, Suslowitz N, Cuccaro ML, Haines J and Pericak-Vance M (2010) Prevalence Rates of Autism Spectrum Disorders Among the Old Order Amish. *International Society for Autism Research*.

Rodgers J (2022) Autistic people are six times more likely to attempt suicide – poor mental health support may be to blame. *The Conversation*. Available at: https://theconversation.com/autistic-people-are-six-times-more-likely-to-attempt-suicide-poor-mental-health-support-may-be-to-blame-180266 (accessed May 2024).

Rogers S (2016) Adapting CBT for children with an autism spectrum disorder (ASD) [online]. www.bacp.co.uk/bacp-journals/bacp-children-young-people-and-families-journal/september-2016/creative-cbt-with-autism-spectrum-disorder/ (accessed May 2024).

Rumball F (2019) A systematic review of the assessment and treatment of post-traumatic stress disorder in individuals with autism spectrum disorders. *Rev J Autism Dev Disord* **(6)** 294-324. https://doi.org/10.1007/s40489-018-0133-9.

Russel G (2021) *Time trends in autism diagnosis over 20 years: a UK population-based cohort study.* ACAMG. https://acamh.onlinelibrary.wiley.com/doi/10.1111/jcpp.13505

Rusting R (2018) Decoding the Overlap between Autism and ADHD. *Scientific American*. Available at: www.scientificamerican.com/article/decoding-the-overlap-between-autism-and-adhd/ (accessed May 2024).

Sandin S, Lichtenstein P, Kuja-Halkola R, Hultman C, Larsson H and Reichenberg A (2017) The Heritability of Autism Spectrum Disorder. *JAMA*. **318** (12) 1182-1184.

Sedgewick F, Hull L and Ellis H (2021) *Autism and Masking: How and Why People Do It, and the Impact It Can Have*. Jessica Kingsley Publishers.

Sharpe R, Curry W, Brown R and Shankar R (2019) A public health approach to reducing health inequalities among adults with autism. *British Journal of General Practice* https://bjgp.org/content/69/688/534.

Shkedy G, Shkedy D & Sandoval-Norton AH (2021) Long-term ABA Therapy Is Abusive: A Response to Gorycki, Ruppel, and Zane. *Adv Neurodev Disord* **5** 126–134. https://doi.org/10.1007/s41252-021-00201-1.

Slavny-Cross R (2022) Autism and the criminal justice system: An analysis of 93 cases. *Autism Research* https://doi.org/10.1002/aur.2690.

Tanne JH (2002) MMR vaccine is not linked with autism, says Danish study. *BMJ*. 2002 Nov (7373):1134. www.ncbi.nlm.nih.gov/pmc/articles/PMC1124634.

Taylor P (2017) Neurodiversity as a Competitive Advantage. *Harvard Business Review*. https://hbr.org/2017/05/neurodiversity-as-a-competitive-advantage (accessed May 2024).

Waltz M (2015) Mothers and Autism: The Evolution of a Discourse of Blame. *AMA J Ethics*. **17** (4) 353-358. https://doi.org/10.1001/journalofethics.2015.17.4.mhst1-1504.

Wang X, Li X, Guo C, Hu Y, Xia L, Geng F, Sun F, Chen C, Wang J, Wen X, Luo X and Liu H (2021) Prevalence and Correlates of Alexithymia and Its Relationship With Life Events in Chinese Adolescents With Depression During the COVID-19 Pandemic. *Front Psychiatry*. **12** 774952. https://doi.org/10.3389/fpsyt.2021.774952.

Wigdor EM, Weiner DJ, Grove J, Fu JM, Thompson WK, Carey CE, Baya N, van der Merwe C, Walters RK, Satterstrom FK, Palmer DS, Rosengren A, Bybjerg-Grauholm J; iPSYCH Consortium; Hougaard DM, Mortensen PB, Daly MJ, Talkowski ME, Sanders SJ, Bishop SL, Børglum AD and Robinson EB (2022) The female protective effect against autism spectrum disorder. *Cell Genom*. **2** (6) 100134. https://doi.org/10.1016/j.xgen.2022.100134.

Williams KR and Wishart JG (2003) The Son-Rise Program intervention for autism: an investigation into family experiences. *J Intellect Disabil Res* **47** (Pt 4-5) 291-9. https://doi.org/10.1046/j.1365-2788.2003.00491.x

Willingham E (2013) *10 Weirdest Things Linked to Autism* [online]. Available at: www.forbes.com/sites/emilywillingham/2013/09/04/10-weirdest-things-linked-to-autism/ (accessed May 2024).

Zeliadt N (2019) *Sensory overload in autism may stem from hypervigilant brain* [online]. Available at: www.spectrumnews.org/news/sensory-overload-in-autism-may-stem-from-hypervigilant-brain/ (accessed May 2024).